UNEXPECTED
MOMENTS

Unexpected Moments

Daisy Paige

Library of Congress Control Number: 2022903178
ISBN: Hardcover   978-1-6698-1191-6
               Softcover   978-1-6698-1190-9
               eBook   978-1-6698-1189-3

Cover illustration by Lana Faith.

KJV
Scripture quotations marked KJV are from the Holy Bible, King James Version
(Authorized Version). First published in 1611. Quoted from the KJV Classic
Reference Bible, Copyright © 1983 by The Zondervan Corporation

Print information available on the last page.

Rev. date: 03/04/2022

To order additional copies of this book, contact:
Xlibris
844-714-8691
www.Xlibris.com
Orders@Xlibris.com
838618

Dear Reader,

I hope you enjoy my story and that it is able to help anyone in similar situations and know that you are not alone. If you keep praying for God to give you strength to pull you through suffering or difficult times, He will. You must have faith. Some things I have prayed for in my life, I know now that it was by the Grace of God, He always provided for my family and me one way or another. God answers our prayers, they may not be the answers you have hoped for, but he knows what is best and what door to open. Just listen to him or watch for his signs. I believe I went through the things in my life to make me strong enough to face what is ahead. I have forgiven those that have harmed me physically and emotionally, with God's help. Just give it to Him and pray about it. They must repent the sin of the harm that they brought upon you and ask for forgiveness. Remember God only puts you through what he knows you can handle, and he is always there to help you through your **"Unexpected Moments"**. If you believe that Jesus died on the cross to pay for your sins and that he rose from the dead, then there is a place in heaven for you.

God bless you,

Daisy Paige

For God so loved the world that he gave his only begotten son. That who so ever believeth in him shall have every lasting life.

—John 3:16

Foreword

It was an autumn night in Texas when I first met Daisy. She came up in a wheelchair next to me at the campfire. Her smile was bright. She shared her journey with me and told me she did not have much time left on earth. I told her to write down her story and I would do anything I could to help share her story with the world. I only spoke with her briefly that night, but her attitude and resilient spirit inspired me.

I hope this book of an individual's incredible journey through emotional, physical, and spiritual pain and coming through the other side of tragedy still praising the Lord will encourage you in your present situation. Daisy's message will bring you comfort and remind you that you are not alone in your struggles or life's circumstances. I pray her words bring you hope. There is One who knows the plans He has for you, plans to give you hope and a future. (Jeremiah 29:11)

— **Kirk Cameron**

Some of my favorite verses:

But without faith it is impossible to please Him, for he who comes to God must believe that He is, and that He is a rewarder of those who diligently seek Him. **Hebrews 11:6**

When we come to God, we must believe that He is and that He rewards us with what we are praying for. We must believe that He sees us and that He is full of love, care, and goodness. He is aware of all our difficulties, and He bends and turns everything for our good if only we love Him and believe in Him. He has counted all the hairs on our head, and He sees to it that no temptation or trial is too difficult for us.

God will provide a way out.

No temptation has overtaken you except what is common to mankind. And God is faithful; he will not let you be tempted beyond what you can bear. But when you are tempted, he will also provide a way out so that you can endure it. **1 Corinthians 10:13**

Eternal Love

Endless days, sleepless nights,
As we go through our constant fights.
Do we really get what we see?
Or is it totally up to me?
Struggling through our trying times,
Burdened by the price of crimes.
Truly as each day ends,
Know that God's your only friend.
As "Footprints in the Sand" doeth say,
He really carries us all the way.
Know this, for it is up to you.
He already knows what you should do.
Find your faith from heaven above.
Then you will have eternal love.

CHAPTER ONE

On Friday evening, September 1, 1967, Karen Raney and Wade Walden exchanged vows in the Lincoln Street Baptist Church, which was where the bride and groom first met. The Reverend Gary Burke, pastor of the church, officiated the ceremony.

The church was decorated with a single arrangement of gladioli accented with pink satin ribbon. Satin bows marked family pews. The remaining pews were filled with other family members, friends, and high school classmates from Karen's school. Firefighters who worked with Wade and his friends were seated there as well.

The maid of honor was Karen's sister, Leigh. She came down the aisle first wearing a pink lace dress and a tiny hat veiled with tulle. Next were the bridesmaids, Wade's sisters, Elsa and Mary, wearing pink two-piece lace dresses, carrying bouquets of fresh tulips.

Wayne Jr., Wade's brother, was the best man wearing a nice gray suit with a pink boutonniere. Karen's brothers, Carter and Jean, were the groomsmen, also wore gray suits and pink boutonnieres.

Her father, Wesley Raney, wore a gray suit too and happily gave the bride away. She was wearing a handmade gown of white satin, softly imprinted with tulips, fitted lace bodice, a beaded scooped neckline, and satin shoulder bearing capped sleeves, along with a three-tiered veil of silk illusion falling to fingertip length from a satin rose encircled by knitted floral patterns enhanced with starry seed pearls. Her only jewelry was a strand of pearls. She carried atop a white Bible her bouquet of feathered white carnations and pink tulips tied with pink and white satin streamers caught in love knots.

The reception after the wedding was held in the parsonage. The table was covered with white lace over pink linen centered with an arrangement of pink and white tulips. The three-tiered wedding cake was decorated with pink sugar spun roses and topped with the traditional miniature bride and groom.

Everyone enjoyed cake and punch and mingled for a while. Karen visited with her friends and thanked them all for coming. Everyone was so happy for the newlyweds. Wade thanked his coworkers as they all gave him a hard time in fun. Then Wade and Karen left. She wore a pink three-piece suit with a white carnation corsage. Everyone cheered for them as they threw rice at them on their way to the truck. It was going to be their first night as husband and wife and their first night in their home together.

As they lay in bed cuddled in each other's arms, Karen couldn't believe they were actually married. "Can we stay like this forever?" she asked Wade. "This was the best night of my life."

He replied, "It was for me too. I know we will have many more great nights ahead of us." He gave her a soft kiss. "I do like the fact that I get to say *wife* now instead of *fiance*."

Karen said, "And I get to say *husband*. Wow! We did it, Wade, we are husband and wife. till death do us part." She smiled and curled up tighter onto his chest. "Am I dreaming? 'Cause if I am, then I don't want to wake up, and if I'm not, I want to stay like this for eternity!"

"I am so glad that you let me be the man to make you happy. I have loved you for three years, and I intend to continue to make you the happiest woman in the world, Karen. This I promise."

Karen smiled the biggest smile she possibly could and replied, "I want to make you the happiest man in the world."

"Tomorrow I will make my wife breakfast in bed."

Still smiling, Karen said, "I can't wait, husband!" They lay there in each other's arms and fell into a deep sleep.

The next morning, Wade slipped out of bed and went to the kitchen. He had already picked up some groceries and brought them to the house while Karen was getting ready for the wedding. He was going to make her pancakes, scrambled eggs, and sausage. He had orange juice and coffee too.

She smelled the sausage cooking from the bedroom and got up from the bed and put her robe on. She walked into the kitchen, wrapped her arms around Wade, and said, "Good morning, husband!" He said he liked the way that sounded but scolded her back to the bed so he could bring her breakfast. She smiled and ran off back to the bedroom.

When breakfast was ready, he had a tray with a tulip in a vase, a cup of coffee, cup of orange juice, a plate with pancakes and sausage, and a saucer of scrambled eggs. He carried it over to the bed. "I'll be right back with some warm syrup," he said as he ran off and came back with another tray.

After the two finished breakfast, they decided to go for a little drive. After all, the truck was decorated with "Just Married" written on it, and it was too dark for anyone to see it after the reception. They drove around the lake and thought they would go for a walk.

They went over to the picnic table where Wade had proposed, and he took out his knife. "Let's make this our special table." He carved a heart and inside it carved "WW+KW 4Ever!"

"What do you want to do now?" he asked Karen.

"Go home to our house and take a nap," she said laughing.

"Sounds good, my love, sounds good." He helped her back into the truck, and she sat close to him.

"I don't want to go to school tomorrow," she said.

"I don't want to go to work tomorrow either," Wade replied, "but we promised your father you would stay in school. Those were his terms of marriage."

Karen nodded her head. "Wade, I don't want to stay at the house all night alone. You think I can see if someone will stay with me?"

Wade answered, "Of course. That's a great idea."

Five months had gone by since the two had been married. Karen had picked up a side job of babysitting a couple of kids after school to bring in a little extra money. She helped them with their homework and gave them snacks. After that, their parents usually picked them up.

It was Thursday evening, and Wade was home. Karen was a little nervous because she was feeling a little queasy and late for her time of the month. After the kids left, Karen thought she'd better tell Wade.

"Honey, I have something to tell you."

He looked up at her quickly with a worried expression. "What's wrong?" he asked.

"I think I may be pregnant," she said.

"Well, we better find out. Why don't you call and see if you can get an appointment at the doctor's office."

The doctor had an opening first thing in the morning. They would have to wait until the morning to find out. "Oh, Wade, I am not going to be able to sleep tonight. I'm so worried."

Wade took her in his arms and said, "Darling, there is nothing to worry about. We are in this together as husband and wife. If you are, I will be here for you, and we'll be a family." He smiled and told her to go to bed and they'd see what happened in the morning.

The next morning Karen quickly woke Wade up so he could share this experience with her. They went to the doctor's office. Karen took the test and waited for what seemed like the longest time in their lives for the results. When the doctor came in with the test results, Karen closed her eyes.

"Doctor, what do the results say?" she asked him.

He replied, "You're going to be parents!"

She burst into tears. "I don't know how to be a parent!"

Wade said happily, "We're going to have to learn that together. Neither do I."

When they got back home, she ran to the toilet getting sick. Wade went over to get her a cool wet cloth and held her hair back. "Why don't you stay home from school today and take it easy?" he asked her. "Then you and I can both take the weekend to adjust to the idea, and try to get your nausea under control."

She looked up at him, her skin a sickly shade of green. "Okay. I will see if Sam can come keep me company." Sam was her niece but more like a friend being so close in age.

The next morning once Wade arrived home, Sam left to go home. Wade asked his wife how she was feeling.

She responded, "Dry toast has been about the only thing that helps."

Wade went to the kitchen and came back with a tray for her. He had made her toast and a glass of orange juice, and just to be safe, he had included a glass of ginger ale.

"Thank you so much," Karen said as she gave Wade a kiss.

After she ate, she was able to get out of bed without feeling nauseous. The two decided to go to Wade's parents and share the news with them. As they pulled up in the driveway, Elsa parked behind them. "I guess we get to share the news with her too," said Karen.

They managed to get everyone into the living room. "We have some news for you all," announced Wade. Elsa burst out, "Is Karen pregnant?"

Wade peered at Elsa with a tight expression. "Yes, Elsa she is! We haven't told anyone else yet, so keep your mouth shut!" She promised she wouldn't say anything. The family was excited for them, and Liz said she'd help out any way she could.

They had to go tell Mr. and Mrs. Raney. Wade was extremely nervous about Mr. Raney's response. When they drove up to the house, Mr. Raney was out on the tractor. Karen was grateful for that. It meant she could tell her mother first. She stormed the kitchen shouting, "Mother, I have something to tell you. Please don't be upset."

Her mother asked, "What, are you expecting?"

Karen looked surprised as she answered, "Yes, how do you know?"

Mrs. Raney just looked at her, shaking her head. "Call it mothers' intuition." She didn't appear to be mad, but Wade was more worried about Mr. Raney's reaction.

"How do you expect Mr. Raney to react to the news?" he asked her.

"Well, I reckon he'll be a little upset at first, but he'll get used to the idea." About that time Mr. Raney came in for lunch. "Wesley, sit down. I've almost got your lunch ready. The kids have something they need to tell you."

Mr. Raney went to wash up and sat down in his chair at the table. "What's this you need to tell me?" he asked them with a stern face.

Karen answered, "We're going to have a baby, Daddy."

He looked away then back at Karen. "How on earth do you expect to finish school now?" he asked.

"I'm going to do the best I can. I promise, Daddy."

The couple knew Mr. Raney would be okay after a while. Karen wanted to go tell Leigh in person, so Wade drove her over there. Karen knocked on the door, and they heard Leigh announce for them to come in.

"Hi, Leigh," said Karen. "Could you sit down for a minute?" she asked.

"Sure. Just a minute," Leigh answered as she dried her hands off from washing the dishes.

Karen looked at her sister and said, "Wade and I are going to be parents."

Leigh stood up and hugged her baby sister. "Oh, Karen, I am so happy for you both."

Seven months later, not long after their first anniversary, Karen woke Wade up. "Honey, I think my water just broke."

Wade shouted as he stared at her, "What? Are you sure?"

Karen responded, "Yes, everything is wet."

"Ah! Okay. We've got to get to the hospital, now!"

After they got to the hospital and the doctor confirmed she was in labor, Wade started calling the families.

Soon the room was filled with family members who are happily waiting for the arrival of the baby. They were all talking among themselves when Karen screamed out in pain. The nurse asked everyone to please leave the room except Wade.

Twenty minutes later, a healthy baby boy weighing eight pounds thirteen ounces was born. He was twenty inches long. The nurse cleaned the baby up and handed him to Karen. Wade just stared at the two of them in awe.

"He has your eyes, babe," Wade said. "Oh my goodness! I better go tell the family the news."

So much cheering and tears of joy in the waiting room as Wade shared the news.

"What's his name?" asks Celie.

The proud father smiled and said, "We're going to call him J.R. Wade J.R. Walden, but nicknamed him J.R."

The hospital allowed the father and two visitors at a time, so the family knew the proud grandmas should go first.

Celie insisted she got to hold him first. So she went and scooped him up. "Oh, he's such a cutie! He has Karen's eyes and Wade's nose." Celie handed J.R. to Liz. "Whoever thought a baby boy could be so beautiful?" The grandmas shared time with the baby for a bit, then let others come in to visit.

Wesley and Wayne Sr. came in to see their precious grandson. They were both a couple of proud grandpas. Wesley sat down to have his turn holding the precious boy. He had someone hand him over after he was seated as he was afraid of dropping the little one. As a child, he suffered from polio, crippling his left side. After a few minutes, Karen said, "Someone better go get Leigh and Elsa to come in for their time."

Leigh came in first saying, "Hand him over." She swaddled him for a couple of minutes, and he started crying uncontrollably. She handed him to Elsa, but the crying didn't stop. Once Karen had him, he was content.

Elsa told Wade that she would get her turn in later and that they'd better let the little family get some rest. She agreed to tell the rest of the crew in the waiting room that they would just have to wait to get some time to see J.R.. Leigh and Elsa said their goodbyes and were off.

Karen just lay there smiling in amazement, looking at both J.R. and Wade. This was indeed their little family. Wade did the same. There was no need for words. Their smiles said it all.

Wade told Karen to let the nurses take J.R. back to the nursery so she could get some rest. She just didn't want to let go of him. Just holding him close swaddled in his little blanket. That's how she wished they could stay.

She finally agreed with Wade. She was too tired not to. As soon as the nurses took him away, she closed her eyes and was fast asleep.

CHAPTER TWO

Karen and J.R. got to go home two days later. It felt good to be home, thought Karen. She and Wade hadn't quite finished the nursery, but that was okay. After all, J.R. would sleep in their room in his bassinet for a while. Since newborns slept a lot, finishing the nursery would give Karen something to do. Wade would be home for a few days before he would have to go back to work.

The three had not been home too long when there was a knock at the door. Wade went to see who it was. A moment later, Liz came asking Karen where her precious grandboy was. Karen told her she had just put him down for a nap. It gave them a chance to visit while Wade and Wayne Sr. visited in the living room.

"We need to give you a baby shower so you can get the things for J.R. that you need," Liz told her. The two got to planning it out. They would have it here so J.R. could be comfortable in his own home, and Karen would just have to put the things away, not load and unload the car with the gifts.

While the two of them were planning the shower, Wade and Wayne Sr. were planning a day of fishing. "I can't wait until J.R. gets big enough to go fishing," said Wade.

"Hey, slow down. He's not even a week old yet," Wayne Sr. responded. "He'll be grown before you know it."

Wade J.R. woke up crying. "He's hungry," said Karen. Liz offered to hold him while Karen fixed his bottle. She returned to the room and handed the bottle to Liz. "I thought you might like to feed him," she told her.

"Well, of course," replied Liz.

"What's all the fussing about?" Wayne Sr. asked J.R., like he would answer him. "Oh, I see. Somebody was hungry."

Liz stopped feeding halfway through the bottle and put J.R. over her shoulder while she burped him. Out came a loud belch! "Oh my goodness!" exclaimed Liz. She fed him the other half of the bottle and repeated. He belched loudly again. "My! He's a good burper," Liz said as Karen shook her head yes.

"Well, Mamaw, we better get home," Wayne Sr. told Liz.

She handed the baby over to Karen and kissed them both on their foreheads, saying, "Love y'all. Let us know if you need anything."

Karen shook her head yes and told Liz that she loved them too and to come visit anytime she wanted.

A couple of hours later, Celie called to see if they could come over to visit.

"Yes, Mother, you don't have to ask to come visit your grandson," Karen told her as she rolled her eyes. She asked Wade if he could get a bottle ready so that Celie could feed J.R. when they arrived.

Wade went to the door and let Wesley and Celie in. Once inside, Celie made her way back to the bedroom without saying a word to Wade. "There's my boy!" she exclaimed as she took him from Karen's arms. A minute later, Wade walked in with a bottle for him. "Are you sure that's not too hot?" she asked him. "You don't want to burn his mouth."

Wade responded, "Nope, it's just right."

Celie tested it herself before putting the bottle into the baby's mouth.

When the bottle was halfway gone, Karen told Celie J.R. needed to be burped. Celie was offended. "Karen, I think I know how to feed a bottle to a baby. I did raise four of you."

Karen gritted her teeth and looked away before saying, "Sorry, Mother. Sure you do."

About thirty minutes had passed, and Wesley came into the room. He walked over to Karen and kissed her on the cheek asking, "How is my baby girl?"

Karen responded, "I am good, Daddy. Thank you for asking."

"Celie, we need to go home. I've got a busy day tomorrow."

Celie looked down at J.R., saying, "Grandmother will just have to come get some more loving another time. Won't she?"

As they were leaving, she told Karen that she had left a jar of homemade stew and a plate of fresh homemade cornbread on the counter.

"Thank you, Mother. That sounds wonderful for dinner. I will heat up the stew."

After Wesley and Celie left, Karen heated some stew up for her and Wade to eat for dinner. Celie's homemade stew was the best. Once they were done eating, Karen wanted Wade to help her with some ideas for paint colors in J.R.'s nursery. She had picked up some swatches from the hardware store. She'd like to have it painted before the baby shower.

They looked through the swatches and decided on a sea green. Wade would go to the hardware store tomorrow and get the paint and start painting. They had already gotten a crib from Liz. She had a few of them since she watched children at her house as a job. Wade would sand it down and stain it to make it look new. He was good with woodworking, a talent he learned in shop class in high school. She would ask for bumper pads and crib sheets in her wish list for the shower.

Wade went to the hardware store to get the paint for the nursery. He was also going to get some wood to build Karen some shelves for storage. Maybe he'd surprise her and build a changing table too. He got everything he needed to fix the nursery up.

When he got home, he took the wood for the shelves and baby changing table to the back porch. Then he took all the paint and everything else he needed to paint the walls to the second bedroom. He also took the crib to the back porch for sanding and staining.

Wade got started painting the room. About an hour went by, and he was done with the first coat. He would let that dry and see if Karen wanted some lunch.

He popped his head into the bedroom and noticed she was asleep, so he just went into the kitchen and made them both a sandwich, a glass of tea and grabbed some chips. He put it on the tray and took it to the bedroom. "Honey? Are you hungry? I made you some lunch."

She sat up and smiled, saying, "I've got the best husband in the world."

After they ate their lunch, he called her into the nursery to see the walls. He told her that he wanted to add a second coat but asked her if she liked the color on the wall. She agreed it was perfect. J.R. had kept Karen up most of the night. He was sleeping well today, but Karen thought he might need to wake him up for a little bit, afraid he was getting his nights and days mixed up.

Today was Thursday, so they had nine days until the baby shower. Celie would be over later to help her with the invitations. Neither Wade's mom, Liz, nor Celie had ever learned to drive. That left them to rely on others to get them where they needed to go.

Wade was out back working on the shelves when Wesley and Celie pulled up in the driveway. Wesley heard the saw, so he went to the backyard to see if Wade needed help, and Celie made her way inside to see Karen and J.R.. She called out for Karen, but not too loud in case J.R. was sleeping.

"In here, Mother," said Karen from her bedroom. She was feeding J.R.. After she burped him, she handed him over to his grandmother. "Try to keep him awake," she told her. "He kept me up most of the night." Celie nodded her head as she made goo goo noises at him.

Karen began to make a list of people to invite over for the shower next weekend. Celie had picked up some invitations on their way over. In each invitation they would write what they needed for the nursery or baby.

J.R. wouldn't keep his eyes open anymore, so Celie put him in the bassinet. After Karen finished the list, she and Celie went into the dining room to make out the invitations.

Wade and Wesley had finished making and painting the shelves and were in the room adding the second coat of paint to the walls. While that was drying, they went outside to start working on the changing table.

Wesley came inside and asked the ladies if they were going to be a while. They both shook their heads yes. He told them he would run up to Rawleighs and pick up some burgers.

"That sounds yummy, Daddy," Karen said.

While he was gone, Karen and Celie continued writing out the invitations and putting stamps on the envelopes. Celie put the ones aside that she would deliver in person.

Karen heard hammering coming from the nursery, so she went in to see what was going on. Wade was hanging the three shelves that he had made.

"Those are so pretty," she told him.

He said, "I figured you might need the storage room." They heard Wesley say he was back. Wade was going to wash up and meet them in the dining room.

After they ate their meal, Celie picked up J.R. while Karen went to feed him. When she left the room, Wade told Celie about the surprise changing table he was building and asked her if she would make a cushion for it.

"Well, of course I will," she told Wade. She said that would be a nice surprise for Karen.

He went back out to finish staining the crib. He, at least, wanted to get that done tonight so he could put it together in the nursery tomorrow.

When Karen finished feeding and changing J.R., she asked her mother if she would give him a bath while she finished working on the invitations. How could a grandmother say no to that? She quickly snatched J.R. up and took him over to the kitchen sink after gathering his bathing supplies.

Karen finished making out the invitations. Celie was going to drop them off in the outgoing mail at the post office. Wade and Wesley were bringing the crib inside. It would probably take both of them to get it together. Wade would work on the changing table tomorrow.

Karen told Wade she was going to take a shower and go to bed. She was exhausted! So was he. He was also glad he had four more days off to get the changing table ready before he had to go back to work.

It was the day of the baby shower. Leigh and Elsa had arrived early with Celie and Liz to help with getting everything in order. Earlier that morning, Wade had snuck out to bring the changing table into the nursery. Karen had been told to stay out of there until the shower.

There were balloons and streamers decorating the kitchen and living room. A cake was made to look like toy building blocks. The message they made said "Welcome, Wade J.R." There was a table set up for the gifts and a table covered in all sorts of appetizers and finger foods with a bowl of blue-colored punch.

Guests were starting to arrive. J.R. was fast asleep in the bassinet that had been rolled into the living room for everyone to see. Elsa had even decorated it. The cute cozy house looked nicely decorated.

Leigh sat next to Karen with a notepad to take down names and the gifts received. This being Wade and Karen's first child, they didn't have much for the baby boy. They received blankets, diapers in all sizes, crib sheets, onesies, cute little baby boy outfits, a dehumidifier, hats, shoes, burp cloths, bumper pads for the crib, shoes, and some toys.

Once all the gifts were opened, Liz told Elsa to take Karen to the nursery. She covered Karen's eyes until they had the light on and Karen was in the doorway. When she uncovered her eyes, it took everything in Karen not to cry when she saw the changing table Wade had made for her. It was gorgeous! She wondered how he had made this and got it into the room without her knowing it.

J.R. started to cry. Leigh brought him a diaper, wipes, and powder to the changing table and told Karen she should try it out. It was the perfect height. They couldn't have bought one any better. Wade was really good with his hands.

After J.R. was all cleaned up, Celie had a bottle ready for him. She took him from Karen so she could feed him and she could eat and visit with her guests.

Karen went out and asked if everyone saw the changing table that Wade had made for them. If they hadn't seen it, she welcomed them all to go check the nursery out, also told everyone to fix them a plate and be sure to have some cake.

Leigh and Elsa were cleaning up all the wrapping paper and making sure that all the gifts were noted on the pad for Karen so she could thank them.

Wade just happened to walk in before anyone had a chance to leave. He went over to Karen and gently kissed her forehead.

She asked him, "How on earth did you manage to keep that changing table a secret?"

He just smiled at her and said, "I have my ways."

She rolled her eyes and laughed. "You sure do and you are so good to us!"

Guests started to leave. Karen thanked everyone for coming. She, Elsa, and Leigh started putting things away in the nursery and getting it organized. It looked like a baby's room now. So cute and put together.

Wesley came in and said, "It's missing something."

Karen asked, "What's that, Daddy?"

About then Carter walked in with a handmade rocking chair.

"Oh my goodness, how beautiful!" Karen exclaimed.

Karen couldn't wait to put J.R. to sleep in the nursery tonight. "Maybe he will sleep all night," she said, hopefully.

Wade and Karen thanked everyone for their help and gifts. The room finally looked like a nursery. It was absolutely beautiful!

When it was time for J.R.'s nightly feeding, Karen sat in the rocking chair and fed him. After he was done, she burped him and rocked him until he was fast asleep. Wade came in when she was just about to lay him in his crib. How small he looked there, she thought.

Wade held Karen in his arms, and they stood there for a while just staring at J.R., watching him as he slept so peacefully. What a beautiful family they had.

CHAPTER THREE

It was January 1973 now, and J.R. was already four years old. Karen was feeling queasy as she got ready for work. She was an escort truck driver for oversized loads, a company Wade's aunt Dede owned. She ran to the toilet. Oh, no way, she thought, she could make it to work in this shape.

Wade came in, and J.R. was at the table eating breakfast.

"Hey, stinker!" said Wade. "Where's Mom?" J.R. just shrugged his shoulders and continued eating. "Karen, you okay?" Wade asked as he entered the bathroom. He saw how green she looked as she stood over the toilet.

"No! There's no way I can work today. I must have caught a stomach bug from somewhere."

Wade called his aunt Dede and let her know Karen couldn't make it in today. Then he put her into bed and grabbed a trash can so it would be handy for her.

"I'll go get you some ginger ale and dry toast," he told her as he wiped her head with a cool rag. He came back into the room with her toast, ginger ale, and some saltines on a tray.

"Thank you," said Karen as she sipped the ginger ale. As soon as she drank it, she was reaching for the trash can. Looked like she wasn't going to be able to keep anything down.

Wade called his mother and asked if J.R. could come stay over with her, that Karen was really sick.

"Of course he can," she said. "Bring him on over."

He told Karen that he would be back. He was running J.R. over to his mother's house.

Lunchtime rolled around, and Wade asked Karen if she wanted some soup. They thought it was worth a try. She had to try to keep something down. She slowly ate about half the bowl, but then it was in no time that she once again was reaching for the trash can.

"All right, we are going to the doctor. You are going to be dehydrated, if you're not already." Karen moaned, but she agreed to go.

Wade helped her into the truck, and off they went to the doctor's office. They waited in the waiting room for what seemed like a lifetime before she was called back.

The nurse asked Karen, "Is there any chance you could be pregnant?"

Oh, Karen hadn't thought about that. "Yes, I guess I could be," she answered. The nurse went to go order some lab work to be done.

A short time later, a lady that worked in the lab walked in. She took a couple of vials of blood from Karen and said, "All right, we'll run these labs and get back with you as soon as possible." The nurse came in to give Karen something for her nausea. The doctor would be back when the results were in from the lab.

About an hour had passed when the doctor returned. "Well, congratulations, Mrs. Walden, looks like you are going to be a mother. Based on these HCG levels in your labs, it shows you're about eight weeks or so along. We'll get you a prescription for nausea and get you home so you can get some rest."

Karen looked at Wade. "We're going to have a little girl," she told him. "I just feel it. As soon as he said I was going to be a mother, I saw a beautiful baby girl in my arms with the biggest eyes."

Wade smiled at her and asked, "You're not excited a little bit, are you?" She just laughed.

It wasn't long before they discharged her with the prescription for her nausea. They were going to stop by Wade's parents' house to pick up J.R. and share their news.

When they arrived, J.R. was outside playing in the dirt. J.R. loved playing with his dump truck. Since he was occupied, they went ahead and shared the news with Liz.

Wade asked her, "Mom, are you ready for another grandbaby?"

She squealed and went to Karen and hugged her neck. "When are we going to expect this little one?" she asked.

"The doctor says I am about eight weeks along. So that will put her due sometime in August, I guess," answered Karen.

"Did you say her?" Liz reacted.

"I just know, as soon as the doctor said I was expecting, it's a girl!" Karen said matter-of-factly.

The two needed to go by the pharmacy to pick up the prescription. Liz told them to just leave J.R. there. He was having fun in the yard. Karen, at least, wanted to tell him that he was going to have a baby sister.

As they walked out the back door, J.R. came running up.

"Moma, are you feeling better?" he asked her.

"Yes, J.R., I am. That is what I want to tell you. It looks like you are going to be a big brother. Mama's going to have a baby." All J.R. said was "Oh okay, well, I am going to play."

Wade and Karen decided to go to Mr. and Mrs. Raney's house first. Wade got out of the truck. As he started to help Karen out, Celie came over. "Everything all right?" she asked. Karen got out of the truck and looked at her. Right away, Celie knew. "Well, when is it due?" she questioned them.

"Do I have a sign on my forehead that says I'm pregnant?" asked Karen.

"You've got the glow," Celie said.

"The baby will be here sometime in August," Wade replied. "Karen says it is a girl."

Celie stared Karen up and down. "She's right. It's going to be a beautiful baby girl. Now let's go find your daddy and tell him."

They all walked out to the edge of the garden where Wesley was working, and Celie called him to come over for a minute.

"What's going on?" he asked. "Did something happen to J.R.?" Everyone laughed. "Well, I guess if you are laughing, he is okay. What is it then?"

Karen said, "You are going to have a granddaughter."

Wesley just shook his head, smiled, and walked back out to the garden.

It was almost time for the pharmacy to close when they pulled up to the curb. Wade ran in to see if they had time to fill Karen's prescription.

"Sure," said the pharmacist, "I'll have it right out."

It was August, the night before Karen's baby shower. Leigh, Karen, and Elsa were decorating. With Karen due any day now, Wade just didn't want her home alone. J.R. was staying at Karen's parents' house.

Karen was going to check on the cake when her water broke. "Girls, we have a problem!" she shouted from the kitchen.

"What's wrong?" Elsa came on and saw the water on the floor. "Leigh, we have to go to the hospital"

"Okay. I'll go get Karen's bag. Y'all go to the car," she told them.

Karen stopped at the car door. "Oh no!" she exclaimed.

"It's coming now?" asked Elsa. "Tell Leigh to check the cake and take it out if it's ready, turn off the oven," said Karen.

They made it to the hospital. Karen told Elsa to go call Wade. She was already dilated to a six, so it wouldn't be long. After the doctor checked her, Wade came rushing in. "Did I make it?" he asked.

"You did. It shouldn't be long though. She's progressing quickly," Leigh replied.

It was just after midnight when the nurse came back in to check on Karen. "Looks like we can get you to the delivery room and get ready to bring this baby into the world," said the nurse. "I will go tell the doctor she's ready."

Karen was wheeled to the delivery room. It was time for the big moment.

"I want you to give me a big push when you have the next contraction," said the doctor. With that being said, Karen gave it everything she had with that next contraction "Good, Karen, you are doing so good," he said. "One more big push, okay?" Then she pushed on the next contraction.

They all heard a big cry. Karen had given birth to an eight-pound, ten-ounce girl.

This baby was me, and this is where my story begins. My name is Daisy. I am the baby girl Karen knew she was having.

CHAPTER FOUR

Two days later we got to go home from the hospital. Both of us were as healthy as could be. I got to sleep in the bassinet next to my mom. She didn't like being too far from me. Daddy was ecstatic he had a little girl. Now we were the perfect little family.

Celie, my grandmother, came over the first morning I was home. "Where's my baby girl?" she asked as she came into the bedroom. I was in Mama's arms as content as I could be. "I need my baby girl," she said. Mama handed me over. Granddaddy Wesley also came in to see me. J.R. had been with them since kids couldn't visit the hospital, so they hadn't seen me yet.

I had the biggest eyes! Mama knew I would from the beginning. That's how strong of a bond we shared. She always wanted a baby girl ever since she was a little girl, and now she had me. Even Granddaddy was eager to hold me. He asked J.R. if he was ready to meet his little sister.

J.R. came over to me and said, "Hey there, little sister, I'm your big brother, and I'm going to take care of you."

Everyone just laughed and thought that was the sweetest thing they had ever seen. J.R. asked, "Can I hold her?" Daddy picked him up and put him on the bed next to Mama. Then he laid me in J.R.'s arms. I just stared at him.

Wasn't long and Papaw, Wayne Sr., and Mamaw, Liz, had come over to meet me. Mamaw told J.R. it was her turn. She carefully removed me from his lap. Then Papaw peered at me from over her shoulder. Of course he wanted a turn too.

After they all had their turn, Mamaw said to Mama, "There are still all the gifts from the shower in here in the living room to open." She put me in the bassinet, and they all went in there to the gifts. I was tired from all the visiting I had done and slept most of the night.

The next morning more family came to meet me. We had a house full of people over. Everyone kept telling Mama anytime she needed a sitter to let them know. Mama's brother, Carter, and his wife, Kathy, brought their whole family with them to meet me.

Their daughters, Sam and Kerrie, agreed with their brother, Ted, that I looked like a baby doll. Of course I was dressed in a pink lacy dress that had satin bows on it and pink lacy bloomers. Aunt Kathy held me and sang to me when I started to cry while Mama fixed me a bottle.

I wasn't prone to cry much. Only when I was hungry, needed a clean diaper, or wanted Mama. She could tell the difference in each cry too.

Sam and Mama were pretty close, so she knew she was telling the truth when she offered to babysit anytime.

Mama's other brother, Jean, and his wife, Bobbie, stopped by as dark was approaching. They had their two girls, Sara and Denise, with them along with their son, Terrance. Uncle Jean said Terrance had been asking all day when they were going to come see me.

Aunt Bobbie told Terrance to sit in the chair if he wanted to hold me. He was quickly seated with arms stretched out to put me in. Everyone laughed as Aunt Bobbie put me in his arms, holding my head. I opened my eyes and looked up at him with a big, gassy smile.

Terrance said, "Look, she likes me."

Aunt Bobbie said to him, "I believe she is just needing her diaper changed." She took me out of his arms as she lay me on her chest, patting my back.

I let out a grunt and a big burp. Daddy said, "Yep, that's my girl." Aunt Bobbie told Mama that she would change my diaper as she laughed.

Aunt Bobbie took me to the changing table and cleaned my bottom up. She gently kissed my forehead and gave me to Daddy. Mama had just dozed off, so everyone moved into the living room to visit. J.R. and Terrance were playing in his room.

After everyone left, Daddy took me to the changing table and changed my diaper and put me in a comfortable onesie.

He told J.R. it was bedtime and to go put his pajamas on and brush his teeth and that he would come read him a bedtime story.

CHAPTER FIVE

It was a little over five months later, and I had been awake crying most of the night with a cough. When Mama went to pick me up from the bed, she noticed I was really warm, so she took my temperature. She was scared when it read 102 degrees. I also had a very bad cough. She called Daddy at the fire station.

"I'm going to take Daisy to the doctor," she told him. "She's running a 102-degree fever."

He told her, "Yes, take her right away. I will meet you there and pick up J.R."

Daddy met us at the doctor and took J.R. to Mamaw's house and was going to come back to the doctor with Mama. Before he could make it back, they had put me in an ambulance to take me to the hospital. Daddy went into the doctor's office and asked the nurse where he could find Mama and me.

"Mr. Walden," she responded, "I'm sorry to say, Daisy has been transferred to the hospital with double pneumonia."

Daddy found out which hospital I was going to and was quickly out the door. He made it to the hospital and asked a nurse in the emergency room where he could find us.

He was quickly at Mama's side and eager to know what was going on. She told him, "The doctor said if I would have been much longer bringing her in she wouldn't have made it." Daddy hugged and held her tightly. "Oh, Wade, am I a bad mama?" she asked him as tears ran down her cheeks.

"No," he replied, "you are a wonderful mother. We didn't know she was this sick."

A couple of minutes later went by, which seemed like an eternity to

Mama and Daddy. He said, "Mr. and Mrs. Walden, I'm afraid we are going to have to put Daisy in the NICU under an oxygen tent for a few nights, and also try to bring her temperature down. Her oxygen level is very low, and her lungs are filled with infectious pneumonia." Mama fell to her knees crying as Daddy held on to her. "She'll need to stay in the tent for at least a week," said the doctor. "In the meantime, we'll keep an eye on her oxygen level."

Only one person was allowed to stay overnight with me, so of course it was Mama. I was keeping her awake at night because I would cough and cry. That made the alarms beep like crazy. She didn't mind though. If her baby couldn't sleep, neither would she.

J.R. stayed with Mamaw and Papaw. They just lived across the street from the hospital. After the second night, Daddy had taken some clothes for Mama over to their house. He persuaded her to go over there to take a shower and see J.R. for a bit. She told him to call over there if there were any changes.

It was nice—she admitted when she got in the filled tub and began to soak. Only within a couple of seconds she dozed off. J.R. knocked on the bathroom door.

"Mama, are you okay?" he asked her.

She jerked awake. "Yes, J.R., Mama will be out in a minute," she replied.

After her bath, she played trucks with J.R. for a while. Mamaw had fixed her some dinner and told her to sit and enjoy it. She ate quickly and asked Mamaw if she would watch J.R. until Daddy came back. Of course Mamaw said she didn't mind.

Mama came back to the hospital. She'd only been gone for three hours, which seemed a lifetime to her. She felt guilty leaving my side. There had been no changes. I was still running a temperature and a low oxygen level.

After the third night, the doctor came in and told Mama he wanted to take some more x-rays to see if there were any changes in my lungs. They showed very minimal change. He was going to increase the oxygen level in the tent and antibiotic dosage.

Mama asked, "Is this normal for there to be no changes."

The doctor responded, "Everyone is different. I promise we're doing everything we can for her."

Mama nodded her head and stuck her hand in the glove through the tent and held my hand. "My poor baby girl," she cried. "Please get better for Mama." She prayed, asking God to heal her baby girl. She called to give Daddy an update.

There weren't many visitors since visitation was so restricted. Grandmother and Granddaddy came a couple of times. Mamaw and Papaw came about every other day or so. Everyone else was calling. There were a lot of calls both to the hospital and Mamaw's house.

Two weeks went by. Mama agreed to let Daddy spend the night with me, but she was staying at Mamaw's. She was exhausted and didn't care. She rarely left my side. Daddy had to beg her to go take showers, and he brought food to her, which she rarely ate.

The next morning, Mama was back bright and early. She made it in before the doctor made his rounds. That was her plan after all.

When the doctor came in, he said, "We've finally got her temperature to stay lower than 101 degrees overnight for the first time," which was good news. "We are trying to slowly turn the oxygen level down on the tent. Also, I'd like to get some more chest x-rays to see if her lungs are clearer. She still has quite a bit of wheezing."

Finally, after four more weeks, I was able to get out of the tent and just use the tube for oxygen and be moved into a regular room. Daddy had gone back to work. He had to—somebody had to work. Mamaw kept J.R., so he was close to the hospital. Daddy stayed at Mamaw's with him at night when he was off.

Grandmother had Granddaddy bring her to the hospital at least every other day. She was always bringing Mama food and clean clothes.

CHAPTER SIX

I was in a better mood than I had been. Maybe I was just missing being held, and since I was out of the tent, Mama got to love on me. Daddy came up to see me when he was off for a while, so he would hold me too. Seems like I was constantly being held since I had been taken out of the tent.

Aunt Kathy and Aunt Bobbie visited at least twice a week. Dede said Mama could go back to work whenever she wanted and she shouldn't even worry if she'd still have a job or not.

The preacher from the church was coming once a week and said they were praying for me constantly at church. Mama didn't think she was ever going to be able to go home again. She'd forgotten what it felt like to sleep in her own bed.

Daddy sure did miss us too. He'd forgotten how it felt to have his whole family at home under one roof. He couldn't wait for me to get better. J.R. thought he moved in with Mamaw and Mama lived at the hospital.

The doctor came in to check on me. I still had a bad cough but no fever. He told Mama, "I still hear quite a bit of wheezing from her lungs and a lot of congestion. However, I do believe she is finally on her way to recovery."

That was the best news Mama had heard in a while. She called Daddy at the fire station to let him know. Then she called Grandmother. "Thank you, Jesus!" cried Grandmother. Daddy was calling Mamaw.

Mama decided to go spend the day with J.R., and Mamaw would sit with me at the hospital. She and J.R. were playing in the backyard. He went and sat in the wagon and asked her to pull him. When she went over to grab the wagon handle, she noticed a snake in the back of the wagon. "Be very still," she told J.R.. She quickly jerked him out of the wagon right before the snake could strike.

She put J.R. down and told him to go inside the house. She was trembling, but she managed to grab a garden hoe and quickly dispatched the snake.

After that, she dropped to her knees and began to weep. She wondered how she managed to keep it together for so long. She was near losing her baby girl, and now this snake almost bit her son.

Was she a bad mother? She asked God that repeatedly. Was he punishing her for something? Was it because she had broken her promise to her father to stay in school? She felt bad about that every day but wouldn't change a thing. She loved Wade, and she loved more than anything being a mother to this beautiful baby girl and wonderful son, even though she felt like she'd deserted him.

Finally, after being hospitalized for six weeks, I was discharged. Mama finally had her baby girl home. She was going to get to sleep in her own bed for a change. I was nearly six months old and had to have my crib in their bedroom because J.R. had the second bedroom.

Daddy was at work, and Mama called him to tell him we were home. He asked her, "Did you call Dede about going back to work?"

Mama just sat there watching me sleep. Daddy asked her a second time.

Finally she answered, "Yes, I will go back next Wednesday." That would give her a full week with me being home.

CHAPTER SEVEN

I woke up a couple of times during the night coughing but not near as bad. Mama got to sleep more and better than she had in the hospital. Daddy came home from work and asked Mama, "How do you feel about working on Tuesdays and Thursdays when I am off and can be with Daisy?"

Mama was quick to answer and snapped back, "No, I really don't want to go back at all. I want to stay home with her and J.R."

Daddy reminded her, "We really need the money to help pay the bills off. The hospital bill was high, and insurance didn't cover most of it."

Mama was going to fix breakfast for J.R. and get me a bottle ready. She asked, "J.R., do you want cereal or french toast?"

He responded, "Cheerios." Mama was really thankful because she didn't feel like cooking.

Daddy took a shower and joined us all in the living room. "Karen," he started, "I know you don't want to have this discussion about going back to work, but we need to talk about it."

Mama said, "She just got home from the hospital yesterday. I think it can wait. I've already told you that I plan to go back on Wednesday."

There was a knock at the door. Daddy went to answer it. Aunt Leigh had come over to give Mama a hand for the day. Also, she just wanted to get her hands on me. She hadn't gotten to visit the hospital because she had kids and couldn't risk exposure and getting her kids sick.

Mama was going to the grocery store. Daddy took J.R. fishing to get him out of the house for a while.

Aunt Leigh just held me and rocked in the rocking chair, saying, "I'm so glad you are better. You gave us quite a scare, young lady." I lay in her arms content and asleep.

Mama got back from the store. Aunt Leigh put me in the crib and helped Mama unload and put the groceries away. Then they sat in the living room and talked.

Mama told her, "It seems like all Wade can think or talk about is when am I going back to work and how much we need the money right now." She began to tear up. "I know we need the money, but I also know I want to spend time with my baby girl. She just got home." She wiped her cheeks and sniffled. "Leigh, I almost lost her. I don't want her out of my sight. It took everything I had to go to the store just now."

Leigh patted her back and said, "I understand, Karen."

Leigh told everyone goodbye and she would be back tomorrow to help Mama out. Daddy asked J.R., "Are you ready to cook up that fish we caught for dinner?"

J.R. excitedly exclaimed, "Yes! He's going to be so good."

After dinner, Mama told J.R. to go brush his teeth, get ready for bed, and she'd come in so they could read a story and say their prayers.

It was the following Wednesday, and Mama was getting ready to go to work. She cooked J.R. some oatmeal, fed me some cereal. Once she was done with that, she went to the bedroom and got dressed. Daddy was also getting ready to go to work. They usually left about the same time.

This was the first day Mama had worked in over six weeks, and she wasn't ready to leave me. She told J.R. to go brush his teeth and get dressed. She wanted me to look pretty for my first day staying with Grandmother, so she put me in a really cute dress.

It broke her heart. She didn't want to leave me. She was leaving and didn't kiss Daddy goodbye. Instead she firmly said to him, "I have done a lot of thinking and have come to a decision. Today will be my last trip with work, and then I am quitting so I can stay home with my baby girl!"

She slammed the door as she left and told J.R. to get in the car. Then she put me snuggly in my car seat, got behind the wheel, and peeled away as she left the house. Daddy was mad, but he didn't get a chance to respond.

When we got to Grandmother and Granddaddy's house, she told J.R. to go inside while she took me out of my car seat. She held me close, kissed me on the forehead many times as she walked into the house, saying, "Mama loves you so much, baby girl."

She handed me to Grandmother as she told her what had happened. They had a long drive today for work, so she let Grandmother know it would be late when she would be back.

Grandmother said, "That's fine, Karen. You just be careful, and don't worry about Daisy. Grandmother is going to take good care of her."

J.R. went out to help Granddaddy in the garden while Grandmother put me in my high chair in the kitchen to keep an eye on me while she was canning her blackberry jam.

Daddy made it to work at the fire station and called Grandmother to see how Mama was.

She told him, "Karen is not ready to leave this baby that she nearly lost, Wade." She cleared her throat. "It's going to be hard for her to be separated from her for a while now."

Daddy told her he understood what was going on now, but he had no way to talk to Mama. She was on the road escorting an oversized load, round trip 150 miles today.

Dede was happy to see Mama back to work. Mama told her, "Dede I can't do it. I just can't be apart from my baby girl. I almost lost her. I am not ready yet, but I will do this trip. After that, I can't work anymore."

Dede understood and really appreciated Mama for making this trip today. She told her to drive the following truck today. She believed the other girl, even new, could handle the lead. She needed the practice if she was going to be doing it full-time.

They began their drive to a town in Arkansas. It will be a long day. Mama couldn't wait to get back home to me.

As they were getting closer to the destination, the lead driver radioed Mama that she was unsure which direction to take. Mama had taken this trip several times, so she told the driver that she would trade places with her.

The lead driver pulled over on the side of the road as Mama passed the eighteen-wheeler to take her place. Another eighteen-wheeler pulled out onto the road, not seeing the escort vehicle Mama was driving and slammed into her. Everyone got out of their vehicles and ran over to hers.

A homeowner was out on her porch and saw the whole thing, so she called 911. Not long after, a state trooper arrived on the scene. He pulled Mama the rest of the way out of the vehicle, as she was already more than halfway out, laying her head in his lap.

"My head hurts," she moaned.

He responded, "I know, ma'am. An ambulance is on the way."

She looked up at him and asked, "Will you please tell my family that I love them?" Then she passed away.

CHAPTER EIGHT

The truck driver from the company Mama drove for radioed the dispatcher and informed him about the accident and of Mama's passing. The owner, Dede, was friends with my aunt Mary. Dede called her to tell her the tragic news. She lived about an hour from Mamaw's house, so Aunt Mary called Mamaw and told her, that way she could get in touch with Daddy to tell him in person.

Mamaw called Uncle Carter, and he went to tell Grandmother and Granddaddy in person. Mamaw called the fire station and told the firefighter who answered, "This is Liz, Wade's mother. I need for Wade to come to my house as soon as possible please. We have a family emergency."

He replied, "Yes, ma'am, I will let him know."

Uncle Carter had asked Uncle Jean and Aunt Leigh to meet him at Grandmother and Granddaddy's. Once everyone was at their house, Uncle Carter told them all the horrible news. Leigh agreed to stay with Grandmother and Granddaddy so that the men could meet my daddy.

Once Daddy got to Mamaw's, he saw she and Papaw were okay but could tell that she had been crying. He asked, "Mother, what is wrong?" She told him to sit down. He knew whatever she was about to tell him was bad news.

"It's Karen, son, she has been in an accident."

He asked, "Is she all right?"

Mamaw began to cry again. "No, son, I am afraid that she did not make it."

Daddy dropped from the chair to the floor screaming, "No! It can't be. There has to be a mistake!"

Mamaw hugged him tightly as she knelt on the floor. "No, son, I am sorry, but she's gone."

Daddy cried out, "I didn't even give her a kiss this morning or tell her goodbye. She was mad at me when she left. She slammed the door and peeled out of the driveway on her way out. I shouldn't have forced her to go back to work. It's all my fault. How am I ever going to live with myself or look at the kids she left behind?"

Grandmother wasn't handling it well either. She just kept looking over at me on the pallet on the floor, saying, "That poor sweet baby girl. She's never going to know her mother and how much she loved her." She cried hard, and Aunt Leigh held her tightly.

Uncle Carter and Uncle Jean made it to Mamaw's house. Aunt Mary had gotten there too along with Aunt Elsa. They all cried as they saw Daddy's pain. He was only twenty-five years old, widower, with a five-year-old and me, a six-month-old baby. It broke all their hearts, as she was loved by many but mostly from the family she left behind.

Uncle Carter asked Daddy, "Do you want Jean and I to take you to Arkansas?"

Daddy looked up with tears flowing down his cheeks. "Yes. Please," he choked, barely able to speak. The three of them got into Uncle Carter's car and began to travel to Arkansas, where Mama had her accident.

A little more than halfway along their silent trip, they drove by a hearse coming from the opposite direction.

"That was probably her," Carter told Jean. "We should go after it." They turned around and sped off to catch up to the hearse.

When they got up next to the car, they motioned for the driver to pull over. The driver pulled into a gas station and got out of the car.

Uncle Carter got out of his car and went over to the driver. "My sister was just killed in a car accident, Karen Walden. Do you have her?"

The driver responded, "Yes. I am so sorry for your loss. She was so young. You can follow me to the funeral home."

They made it to the funeral home in Texas, and Daddy, barely able to walk, asked, "Can I see her?"

The driver said, "Sir, no disrespect, but I don't recommend that. It's not good."

Daddy cried out, "Of course it's not good, she was my wife. We have two kids. I need to see her. I need to see that she is really gone. I do not believe it."

The driver went to the back and pulled her out. Then he unzipped the bag.

"No, Karen, darling, you can't leave me!"

Uncle Carter and Uncle Jean had to hold him up as all three of them cried.

They managed to get Daddy back into the car and take him over to Mamaw's. Once they helped him into the house, they went to Grandmother and Granddaddy's house. Aunt Leigh was still there, as were quite a bit of relatives who had heard the news. Everyone cried as they held me or looked at me. They tried to grieve as quietly as possible because J.R. still did not know that he would never see our mother again.

"Why?" asked Grandmother. "Why did my baby girl have to die and leave these babies without a mother?"

No one could understand it. It was indeed a very sad situation. Now Daddy had to explain to his little boy that our Mama would never come home again.

CHAPTER NINE

J.R. and I stayed the night with Grandmother, and Leigh did too. Early the next morning, Daddy came over and told J.R. to sit down beside him.

He said, "J.R., your mama went to heaven to be one of Jesus's precious angels." His voice quivered. "He needed her more there for a very important mission."

J.R. asked, "Will she get to come back home when she finishes her mission?"

Daddy teared up as well as Grandmother and Leigh. "No, it is a forever mission, son."

J.R. ran outside as he screamed, "That's not fair! I need her here more!"

Everyone broke into tears as Daddy got on his knees and prayed, "Dear God, please help me have the strength to help J.R. through this."

Daddy, Uncle Jean, Uncle Carter, Grandmother, Granddaddy, and Aunt Leigh had made the arrangements. The obituary read,

> Karen Marie Walden, 23, died Wednesday morning in an automobile accident. Services will be at 2:00 PM Monday, in the Memorial Chapel with the Rev. Roy Farrell officiating. Burial will be in the City Cemetery under the direction of West Funeral Home. Survivors include her husband, Wade L. Walden; a son, Wade (J.R.) Walden; a daughter, Daisy Walden; her parents, Mr. and Mrs. Wesley Raney; a sister, Leigh Breaman; two brothers, Carter Raney and wife Kathy, Jean Raney and wife Bobbie.

J.R. was at the service, but I stayed home, and Sam was babysitting me. After all, a funeral wasn't a place for a six-month-old baby. I'm sure my presence would have made everyone more emotional.

After the services, everyone went over to Mamaw and Papaw's to eat and visit. Sam drove me over there too so that everyone there could get a chance to visit with me. A lot of the family and friends there asked to hold me. Several said that I may have lost my mama, but I had a lot of family and friends who loved me. Everyone volunteered to watch me and J.R. anytime a sitter was needed.

A guest book was on a table by the door. Not only did people sign it and leave condolences, but also they left their phone numbers to call if needed. Mama meant a lot to so many people. This was hard for all of them.

It had been five days since I had my mama hold me. There had been times when I was inconsolable. Mamaw knew it was because I was missing my mama. There was a bottle of bath oil she used. When Mamaw gave it to me, I stopped crying because it smelled like her. She had to give it to me during everyone's visit. No one could hold me. I just kicked and screamed uncontrollably. Neither Daddy, Grandmother, nor Mamaw could stop me from fussing. This broke Daddy's heart. He didn't know how we were going to manage with Mama gone. He couldn't do it by himself.

"Why don't we move you all in here?" Mamaw asked Daddy. "That way when you work on Mondays, Wednesday, and Fridays, I can watch the kids," she told him. "Celie will probably want them some too, and you know there is more than enough room for you all here." Mamaw's house was huge. It was two stories, and there was a second kitchen and living room upstairs.

Daddy told her he would think about it. He thought to himself that this was really the only option because there was no way he was going to stay in our house again without Mama. He would see her everywhere and miss her in their bed at night. He had really already been staying with Mamaw since I had been sick, and I had just gotten out of the hospital two weeks ago.

He kept thinking of the morning she was killed. How mad she was at him. She didn't even give him a kiss goodbye that morning. They really hadn't been the same since I got out of the hospital. Gosh, how he missed her. He was going to blame himself every day for her death. Had she wrecked because she was not thinking clearly since she left that morning mad?

He picked me up and took me to the bedroom and laid me down on the bed. He grabbed his gun from the top of the dresser and crawled onto the bed. He lay me on his legs and put the gun to his head with his finger on the trigger.

"I'm sorry, baby girl, but I can't do this without your mama!" he cried.

Mamaw walked in just in time. "Wade, what are you doing?" she asked. "Do you want both of the kids to not have either parent? We will all help you. It will get easier as time goes on."

CHAPTER TEN

About four months later, Loise, Aunt Leigh's daughter, worked with a lady named Jolie. It had not been long ago that Jolie lost her fiancé in the war. She made plans for Daddy and Jolie to meet at her house for dinner.

Loise's husband and Daddy got along great, so she thought it would work out. Jolie arrived first. When Daddy got there, she introduced them and told them that dinner was ready. Everyone sat down at the table to eat.

"This casserole is so good, Loise, you have to give me the recipe," said Jolie.

There was great conversation at the table between Jolie and Daddy. Loise sat back in her chair and smiled. Had she succeeded in setting the two up?

After dinner, they all went into the living room and sipped on wine as they played charades. Loise had intentionally made Daddy and Jolie partners. They were winning too.

Since they had been drinking, Loise told Daddy to call Mamaw to tell her he'd be home in the morning. She didn't mind. She was glad Daddy had gotten out for some fun.

Loise and her husband went to bed, leaving the two up alone. "One of you can sleep on the couch and the other in the bedroom," she told them.

Daddy shook his head and smiled. That was the first smile Loise saw on his face for as long as she could remember.

Daddy and Jolie sat on the couch drinking wine and talking until they realized it was morning. They had a lot to talk about. Daddy felt comfortable talking to Jolie. He asked her, "Can I kiss you?"

She replied, "Please."

He let her know that he was not ready for a relationship, but he just had the urge to give her a kiss. She told him that she understood.

Loise woke up shocked to see that Daddy and Jolie were still awake. "Can I make you breakfast and coffee?" she asked them.

"That sounds wonderful," Daddy replied.

After breakfast, Jolie said she'd better get home. Daddy walked her to her car and said, "Can I ask you something?" Jolie shook her head yes. "Will you go out with me tonight? Maybe just dinner and bowling?"

Jolie answered, "That sounds nice." She gave him directions to her house.

"I will pick you up at six."

She smiled and said, "I can't wait."

He went back inside. "Loise, I have to admit, before I got here last night, I told myself that there was no way this would go anywhere. I really like her. She is so easy to talk to. I asked her to go out with me, and I am picking her up at six. So I'd better go home, see the kids, and get a nap in."

Mamaw was in the kitchen when Daddy made it home.

"Mother, do you have a moment to talk?"

She was just giving J.R. his breakfast. "Of course, son, what is it?"

He took me out of my high chair after he washed me up and held me tightly. "Is it wrong or too soon to be dating?"

Mamaw looked at him as her jaw dropped and asked, "You like this girl?"

Daddy smiled and answered, "I really do. She is very easy to talk to. We stayed up all night talking. I asked her to go out tonight, if that is okay. I can see if Mr. and Mrs. Raney want the kids for a couple of nights, if you want?"

Mamaw said, "I think Celie would like for them to stay with her for a couple of nights."

Grandmother was beside herself. Daddy didn't usually get the chance to ask her if she wanted us to spend the night. She was the one who always called asking for me and J.R. to spend the night with her.

Daddy and Jolie had been dating for a couple of months, so he introduced us to her. I connected to her right away. We even stayed a couple of nights with her while Daddy worked. Her parents just adored us. J.R. got to ride the horses, so he liked to go over there.

Jolie's dad, John, took me to see the horses. I really liked that. Jolie's mom, Pauline, was a great cook. She managed to get me to eat some vegetables that Grandmother and Daddy couldn't.

Daddy came to pick us up from Jolie's one morning. John was outside and asked him if they could talk for a bit. He told Daddy that he was so sorry for what he had been through with me and J.R.. He also told him that he, Pauline, and Jolie loved us already and he didn't want anyone to get hurt.

Daddy told him, "Those kids have lost so much already that they will never get back. I never thought I could love anyone again after losing Karen. However, I see Jolie with those kids and how much they already love her, and I do too."

John stared at Daddy in awe. "I can tell Jolie loves you too. She is so young to be taking on such a big package, but it makes her happy."

Daddy responded, "How do you feel about me asking her to marry me?"

He gulped. "I think she would love that. If that is what you want, then I will support you. I will accept your children as my grandchildren." Daddy thanked him, and John gave him a hug and patted his back. "You are a good man, Wade. I would be honored to have you as my son-in-law."

Daddy went inside to gather our things and take us home. I was so happy to see him. I took my first steps as I went to him.

"Look at that! She's walking," he said. "Hey, stinker! Are you ready to go home?" he asked.

I reached for Jolie, saying, "Mama!" Everyone teared up, especially Daddy. Inside he wished it was Mama hearing me say that to her. He handed me over to Jolie and asked John if he could talk with him outside for a minute.

As they went out, I hugged Jolie and called her Mama again.

J.R. screamed, "That's not Mama!" He ran out of the room.

Pauline went after him. "J.R., Daisy was so young, she doesn't remember your mama."

He just stared at her and said, "Well, I remember her, and Jolie is not my mama! I want my daddy, and I want to go home."

CHAPTER ELEVEN

Daddy told John he was going to go home and talk to his parents about marrying Jolie. Then he also wanted to go to Karen's parents and let them know before he bought a ring and proposed.

"Thank you for agreeing to allow me to ask her."

We got back to Mamaw and Papaw's house, and Daddy put me down so he could show them I had learned to walk. "Yay!" They clapped as I kept walking. I was proud too. Then I looked up at Daddy and said, "Mama?" His eyes went wide as he told them I was calling Jolie Mama. He told them about the talk he had with John and that he wanted to ask Jolie to marry him. He wanted their thoughts on it first, and of course he would talk to Celie and Wesley too. Mamaw told him she could tell he was happy again, and she saw how Jolie was with me and J.R.. Papaw thought so too. They agreed to watch us while he went to talk to Grandmother and Granddaddy.

Daddy pulled into Grandmother and Granddaddy's driveway. Granddaddy was on the tractor but saw Daddy, so he came into the house. Grandmother met him at the door.

"Is everything okay?" she asked him. It was unusual for him to come over without us.

"Yes," he answered her. "I just need to talk to the both of you." He cleared his throat nervously. "I have been dating Jolie. She is so good to the kids, and they really like her. I wanted to let you know that I plan to ask her to marry me."

"Oh," replied Grandmother as she grabbed her chest. "I knew one day that you would go on with your life, but so soon? Why? Karen hasn't been gone for even a year yet."

Daddy knew this was how she would respond. He looked at Granddaddy.

"You've got to go on living for those kids, and if she makes you happy and treats Karen's babies well, then I don't see what the problem is. Karen would want you to go on living."

Daddy held out his hand and thanked Granddaddy.

"Well, she better not keep me from seeing my grandkids," was Grandmother's worry. Daddy assured her that she wouldn't, but he needed them to agree on one thing.

"What's that?" asked Grandmother.

"You let me be the one to tell Daisy about Karen. When she's old enough and ready, I want to be the one to tell her. I guess I should tell you, she has called Jolie Mama."

Once again, Grandmother grabbed her chest. "I wasn't ready to hear that, but I understand."

CHAPTER TWELVE

It was September 1974 and had been a little over six months since Mama had passed away. Today Daddy and Jolie would marry, and we would all become a family. Not only was she marrying my daddy, but she was choosing to become mine and J.R.'s bonus mother.

J.R. was the ring bearer. Sandy, Jolie's niece, was the flower girl because I was too little, but I still wore a dress that matched the flower girl's.

I was sitting on Mamaw's lap when the bridal party came down the aisle. As soon as I saw Jolie, I screamed loudly, "Mama!" Everyone was awed and thought it was sweet, although it tugged at heartstrings and brought tears to most eyes. Grandmother and Granddaddy were present, and you could hear her cries over the other wedding guests'.

During the reception, I walked around smiling and saying "Hi!" to everyone. Pauline came over and picked me up and said, "Now you can call me Memaw, sweet little one."

I smiled at her, put my hand on her face, and said "Memaw!" with a laugh. She laughed too and gave me a hug. Then she handed me to John.

He said, "You can call me Pepaw."

I laughed, gave him a kiss, and said, "Pepaw!" That just tickled them so. They both said at the same time, "Man, she is so smart." I wanted to get down to go on visiting other guests. Pepaw put me down, and I took off.

I went to see Grandmother and Granddaddy next. I couldn't call them by name as it was too long. I gave Grandmother and Granddaddy a kiss and moved on. I was quite the social butterfly. Anytime someone wanted to take my picture, I was sure to pose.

Daddy and Jolie, who I can only refer to as Mama from here, were going around thanking everyone for coming and saying their goodbyes. They were getting ready to go to Florida for their honeymoon.

Daddy's truck had received the full "Just Married" decor. There were streamers with cans tied to them, "Just Married" written on the back window in shoe polish, wife on passenger window and husband on the driver's side. Everyone threw rice at them as they ran to the truck. Daddy opened the driver's door, and Mama scooted in. He climbed in beside her, and they drove off with Daddy honking his horn.

J.R. and I were going to stay with Mamaw and Papaw for the week while Daddy and Mama were gone. Papaw took J.R. and Aunt Elsa's sons, Joe and Perry, camping for a few nights. Aunt Elsa came and stayed with me at Mamaw's house. We had fun dancing and playing dress-up. That was my new thing. If I saw a camera out, I was going to dance or pose. Aunt Elsa loved taking my pictures and dressing me up, after all, she didn't have any daughters. I was like a daughter to her.

Grandmother called every day to check on me. Every day she got the same reply: I was fine and just showing off every day. She asked if Granddaddy could bring her over to visit me.

"Of course," Mamaw answered, "you are welcome anytime."

Daddy and Mama were on the road heading back from their honeymoon. Grandmother was visiting me when Daddy called Mamaw to let her know. Grandmother told her to ask if she could take me home with her for the night. Daddy told her yes, and she grabbed me up quickly, kissing my cheeks.

Papaw said he would take me and my car seat to their car. He had prickly whiskers and loved to give me pokey kisses with them. That was what he did right after he buckled me in.

CHAPTER THIRTEEN

Three years later, J.R. being nine and me four, Mama had a baby girl. Her name was Anna. I loved her immediately. J.R., not so much. He saw her as coming between him and Daddy. Because Anna would be their biological daughter.

I still thought of Jolie as my mama, so it didn't matter to me. Another reason J.R. was jealous was because Anna was born six days before his birthday, and that meant he'd have to share that special time with her as well.

I was always trying to give her my toys and asking to hold her. Anytime someone came to visit her and take a picture, I made sure to be in it too.

J.R. was in school, and every morning I was up to see him get on the big yellow bus.

"Mama? Why can't I go to school too?" I asked.

She replied, "You aren't big enough yet. Next year you can go."

I stood on my tiptoes and cried, "See, I am too big enough."

She laughed as she said, "Not yet you aren't. Besides, I need you to help me with Anna."

I huffed, "Oh okay, if you need help, I'll stay with you."

Grandmother and Granddaddy were janitors at the church we went to up the road from our house. Most times after they had cleaned it, they'd stop by to see me and J.R.. Since it was usually a weekday, they'd see if I wanted to go home with them for a night or two. I usually cried no unless J.R. was able to go too.

Whenever it was close to time for the bus to drop J.R. off, Mama would call me over to her. She'd put my shoes on, and I had a special spot where

I would wait for him to get off the bus. The bus diver was always so nice and waved at me, saying hello.

J.R. would always take off running from me. "One day I'll be big like you, and I am going to beat you in the race!" I yelled sometimes. There were other days I would cry and tell him that he was mean.

Mama would fix us a snack when he'd get home. Maybe that was why I liked waiting for him. I knew we were about to get something good to eat.

J.R. always had to do his homework after snacks, so I had to leave him alone. When he finished his homework, he'd ask to go outside. That usually meant across the street in the woods where he had built a clubhouse or sometimes next door to Pepaw and Memaw's house. If he went to their house, he either helped Pepaw in the pasture or rode horses. I was too little to do that too. I was always wishing that I would be big so I wasn't always getting told no.

About the only fun outside thing I got to do was ride my bicycle with training wheels in front of the car as Mama drove slowly to Mamaw's house and back. J.R. got to do everything, and I was always jealous. I couldn't wait until I was big like him so I could do fun stuff too.

Chapter Fourteen

The following year came, and I could finally go to school. The happiest memories I had of that time were when we got to drink chocolate milk in class and take a break. That and recess were my favorite things about school. I hated nap time! We had to get our mats out and lay on the floor while the teacher walked around and made sure our eyes were closed. It wasn't always as much fun as I imagined. The big kids on the bus always called me "frog eyes" because of my big eyes. They were also mean to J.R. and called him "blockhead."

One day at recess when I was swinging, this girl walked out in front of me, and I kicked her by accident. She thought I did it on purpose and grabbed me to stop my swing, which pushed my face into the chain and gave me a black eye. I went to the nurse, and she put an ice pack on it. When I got home and Mama saw my eye, she called Daddy. He was mad and called the girl's parents. That made things worse for me at school. Everyone called me "tattletale." I really didn't have any friends and always played by myself or would swing all recess if one was available.

My teacher wasn't very nice either, so I just stayed to myself and did what she asked to stay out of trouble. Lunchtime was another fun time at school. I didn't bring my lunch much because I liked the cafeteria food. Pizza was an all-time favorite for everyone.

Now that I was in school, I missed staying home with Mama and Anna. It was more fun there. At least I got to play with my toys and watch TV.

I would always say I didn't feel good when Mama would wake me up for school. If she made me go to school, I would go to the nurse and say

I didn't feel well. Sometimes I did get to go home, and other times the nurse would give me a Jell-O and make me go back to class after I ate it.

I loved the weekends. I would go stay with Mamaw and Papaw as much as possible. If I didn't stay with them, I would go to Grandmother and Granddaddy's house. Just getting away for the weekend was nice. The only bad thing about staying at Mamaw and Papaw's was when he would hold you down and give you pokey kisses with his whiskers. They had a school bus that they turned into a camper, and we would stay at the lake on most of the weekends. I thought that was the coolest thing ever!

I would also stay at Memaw and Pepaw's if my cousin Tommy stayed over. We would ride horses or play in the barn. Pepaw had a lot of horses and cows. He was building a big shop so that he could work on his tractor or any of his vehicles. He had put barbed wire around it to keep the cows and horses off the foundation. One day I tripped and fell into the barbed wire. Pepaw pulled me off, and I ran into the house crying and bleeding. Memaw was able to fix me up. It just looked worse from the blood than it was.

CHAPTER FIFTEEN

I am eight years old now. My Papaw had become very ill and was in and out of the hospital all the time. I tried to visit as much as possible. Aunt Elsa and her sons, Joe and Perry, had moved in with them and lived upstairs. She babysat kids during the week after school. If I didn't have school, I stayed with her so I could play with Misty. She and I had become good friends.

Aunt Elsa had this awesome marionette bird that we loved to play with. We liked to make it walk up and down the hallway. Misty got to spend the night sometimes, and Aunt Elsa played dress-up with us. It is so much fun.

I loved to stay with Aunt Elsa so I could visit with Papaw while he was awake. One day I went to eat breakfast with him, and he told me to go look in his bedroom closet, that he had something for me. I took off running to the closet, and there was a box on the floor.

I took it to him and asked, "Is this it?"

He replied, "Yes. It is a pocket fishing pole."

I laughed. "No, it isn't. It doesn't fit in my pocket."

He laughed back and said, "Well, it folds up, so it is easy to carry around." I gave him a big hug and didn't mind those pokey kisses he always gave.

Daddy came and picked me up the next morning when he got off work. When we got home, Mama said we were going to have to go spend the night with Memaw and Pepaw. She and Daddy were going to town because Papaw had to go to the hospital. Even J.R. had to stay with them, and he never stayed over there.

J.R. and I took my pocket fishing pole and went crawdad fishing in the ditch out front. We caught so many that we used them for bait. We then rode the go-kart to the pond in the pasture to catch fish. J.R. always scared me when he drove really fast over the hills. The bait worked like a charm. We caught so many that we almost filled a five-gallon bucket with them.

Pepaw said if we caught enough, he would help J.R. clean them and we'd have fish for dinner. We got excited, so we loaded up the go-kart and took the fish to Pepaw. He was shocked that we caught so many. He showed J.R. how to clean them. Then he and Memaw cooked them for dinner.

We ended up staying a couple of nights there before Mama and Daddy came back to get us. Daddy looked really sad when he came inside. I asked, "What's wrong, Daddy?" He told me we would talk when we got home.

When we got home, Daddy told us to come into the living room and sit down. He looked so sad, even had tears in his eyes. He said, "Papaw passed away this morning."

I'd never heard that before. So I asked Daddy, "What does that mean?"

He said, "He went to heaven to be one of God's angels. He's going to be watching you and protecting you from heaven."

I stared blankly at Daddy and asked, "When will he be back?" Daddy just broke down into tears.

Mama said, "He's not coming back. God needs him to live in heaven."

I went and grabbed my fishing pole he gave to me. I told Daddy, "He gave this to me the last time I saw him. Doesn't he need it in heaven?"

Mama replied, because Daddy couldn't, "No, he left it for you to remember him."

I was so upset I cried all day. I loved my Papaw so much. I didn't like that I was never going to get to see him again. This was my first experience with death, or so I thought. I was so upset that I slept with Mama and Daddy that night. Daddy let me keep the fishing pole close.

CHAPTER SIXTEEN

A year had passed. J.R. and I were spending a lot of time at Grandmother and Granddaddy's house. He would push me in the wagon as I steered using the handle. There was a big hill in the front yard that he would pull me to the top of. Giving me a good shove to start me downhill, I would steer frantically to keep control, sometimes turning the wagon over on its side if I turned too sharp.

Uncle Jean had a granddaughter named Lisa that would come over to Grandmother's when I was there. We would also play with the wagon on the hill or the tire swing. We liked to play house and use the screened-in porch as the house.

One day we were playing like it was Christmas, and we had a pine tree limb that looked like a little tree. We were decorating it. I thought a magnolia flower would make a great topper, but when I went to pick it, there was a bee inside. I ran backward but fell, and the bee stung me on my eye.

I ran inside to Grandmother screaming. She put ice on it and told me to lie on the couch. Lisa stayed close by and kept asking if I was okay. I told her I wanted to go home. We didn't know it, but I was having an allergic reaction. I told Grandmother to call my mama so I could go home. I hated to leave Lisa, but I did not feel well at all.

Mama came to get me and brought some Benadryl with her. She asked me if I wanted to stay after I took the medicine and sleep it off. I stayed so I could spend more time with Lisa. We hardly ever got to see each other.

I slept for a couple of hours then woke up feeling much better. Only my eyelid was quite swollen. Lisa and I watched "Family Feud," standing next to a TV tray acting like we were on the show. We also liked to watch

"Wheel of Fortune" with Grandmother. If we weren't watching games on TV, we were playing Aggravation, a game with marbles. We all loved to play that game, especially Granddaddy.

The next afternoon Lisa's mom, Sara, came to get her. Little did I know that this would be our last weekend together. Sara was moving to Tennessee. I didn't want her to go, nor did she want to go.

That afternoon, I couldn't help staring at this woman in a big picture that hung in their living room. It looked as if her eyes followed you. When Grandmother came into the room, I asked, "Who is the woman in that picture?" Grandmother said nothing. She just quickly left the room.

A few minutes later, Mama and Daddy drove up in the driveway. Daddy came in, but Mama sat on the hood of the car.

"Hi, Daddy!" I said as he came in. "I'm not ready to go home yet." He told me to come over to the couch and sit in his lap, that he had something he needed to tell me.

After I sat down, he said, "That lady in the picture was your mother. She has gone to heaven to be with the angels and watch over you."

I immediately ran out to the car and grabbed Mama by her legs. Hugging them tightly, I said, "Mama, please go tell them that you are not dead. They think you went to heaven like Papaw."

Mama teared up as she stood up. Daddy came out to the car. He said, "Mama didn't carry you in her belly. The lady in the picture, named Karen, did. She is your real mama."

"No, that can't be. I don't remember her. Mama is my mom."

Daddy's eyes teared up as he said, "I know you don't remember her. You were just a little baby when she died in a car wreck."

It kind of made sense now. Was this why I felt adopted at times? Was this why Mama couldn't answer me when weeks before I had asked her if I kicked a lot when I was in her belly?

Daddy said, "Karen was yours and J.R.'s mother."

That made me think. I had never heard him call her Mama. "Is it okay that I call you Mama? Even though you're not?" I asked her.

"Of course it is. I love you just like I would if you were my own. You are my daughter."

I hugged her and said, "Please don't leave me and go to heaven too."

She replied, "I'm not going anywhere if I can help it."

We all held hands and went into the house. Grandmother was crying sitting in her chair.

Daddy said, "Your real mother was Grandmother's baby girl."

She stood up and asked, "Would you like to see more pictures of her?"

I shook my head and followed her to the back bedroom. She pulled a big photo album out of a box under the bed as she said, "I've waited a long time to show these to you."

Now it all made sense. I had an extra set of grandparents. I thought they were Mamaw's parents. They were older after all.

I stayed the night with Grandmother, and she was so happy to finally tell me stories about my mother as she showed me pictures. It was so unreal to learn all this in one night. Uncle Carter and Uncle Jean were her brothers. Aunt Leigh was her sister.

The next morning after breakfast, Granddaddy took us to the cemetery and showed me where Mother was buried. It was there that reality set in and I broke down, feeling a big sense of loss.

CHAPTER SEVENTEEN

A year later, and staying at Mamaw's was not the same without Papaw. Aunt Elsa had moved downstairs with Mamaw. Perry slept upstairs, and the other bedrooms were left for guests. J.R. and I liked playing upstairs. Anna didn't like to sleep over. She was a mama's baby.

One day J.R. asked me to go upstairs to play. We went into one of the guest rooms, and he closed the door. Something didn't feel right. I had on pink corduroy overalls. He came over and unbuttoned them, pulling them down, while he pushed me down on the bed. I began screaming loudly. Aunt Elsa came into the room as J.R. was backing away and I was buttoning my overalls.

She held my hand and told J.R. to go downstairs to the living room. I was crying and trembling as she and I walked, still holding her hand to the living room. When we made it there, she told J.R. to get on his knees in front of the couch and we were going to pray about this.

Aunt Elsa said nothing else about what had happened. She thought of it to be just some childhood curiosity. Nothing was said to Mama when she picked us up. The ride home was super-quiet. Things felt different between me and J.R. too.

The next day I was outside on the porch riding my big wheel. J.R. came out there and followed me to the end of the porch. There he looked me in the eye and asked, "It's your fault our mama died, you know? If you would have never been born, she'd still be alive."

I asked, "How was it my fault? I was just a baby."

He then replied, "You were sick and in the hospital, so she missed work for two months. If you would have never been born, she wouldn't have missed work. That's why I am mean to you, so get used to it!"

I rode away on my big wheel in tears. I didn't want anybody to see me crying, so I just went to my room to draw. I loved to draw, and it kept my mind busy.

Anna asked me what was wrong. I told her, "Nothing. I just wanted to draw." Now that she was five we played together more. If I was with her, J.R. wasn't mean to me.

We went to church every Sunday. Mama played the piano. I loved to sing old hymns and go to Sunday school. I participated in Bible drills, read my Bible every day. I rarely missed church on Sundays. I made second place in the regional Bible drill. I could tell you what chapter a verse was if you recited it. I loved reading and studying the Bible. I couldn't believe what was happening to me as much as I believed in and loved God.

There were times when Daddy was at work overnight on his twenty-four-hour shifts and Anna was very much asleep. J.R. would come into our room and do things to me. This went on for four years.

Since Aunt Elsa didn't say anything to anyone, I didn't think I was supposed to either. I never went upstairs alone with him at Mamaw's house again.

Pepaw's aunt Sarah had a granddaughter my age, named Kaye. I would go stay with her as much as possible to be away from home.

I thought Mama knew what was going on. After all, she never let us stay home alone with him. Anna and I would stay at Memaw and Pepaw's house until she got home from work.

I was relieved to see him join the military after he graduated from high school in 1987. Anna moved into his room when he left. We finally had our own rooms and privacy. He had continued to be mean to me until then. I had never said anything. Except to Kaye, we had become quite close.

We went to church camp every summer and always loved our time together. That year at camp, we had a bonfire and sang hymns while roasting marshmallows. I got stung on my hand. At the time I didn't think much of it, but when the bonfire was over and we got into the light, Kaye noticed my neck was swelling. Then when we got into more light, she said my face was too. We found a counselor just in time because I started having trouble breathing. I got to the cabin and lay down, shaking every now and then. Finally, the nurse came in and gave me some Benadryl. She said I was in shock. I asked to use the restroom, and several of the girls got on the counter with towels covering the mirror. They said I shouldn't see myself.

When I went into the stall, I noticed welts all over my stomach. The nurse stayed in the cabin and monitored me all night.

The next morning I felt better. Only my eyes were puffy and almost swollen shut. Kaye let me wear her sunglasses, and we went to breakfast. After we got our trays and sat down at a table, a counselor came by and told me that I had to take off my sunglasses while inside. I took them off, and with wide eyes she told me it was okay to leave them on.

CHAPTER EIGHTEEN

It's September of '87 now, and I am in the ninth grade. I really liked this boy that rode our school bus home. His name was Harry. One day he asked me to sit with him, so I did. We talked the whole time until we got to my house. I was so surprised that he had asked me to sit with him.

The next day Harry asked me to sit with him again. On this day he asked me to be his girlfriend. I couldn't believe it. I had not really ever had a boyfriend. We held hands, and he even kissed me before I had to get off the bus.

We really never saw each other much since he was a grade above me. He would hold my hand in the hall at school and walk me to class. We would sit together on the bus and kiss a lot. Harry would call me when he got home, and we would talk on the phone a few times every night.

There was a really bad snowstorm, and school was closed. It had been a week since I had seen Harry. He called me one day while Mama was gone and asked me to come over to his house so we could see each other and watch MTV videos. The roads were still kind of bad, but I really wanted to see him. I told him to come get me but to be very careful. I wished we could just see each other at my house, but Memaw lived next door and watched to see if anyone came over.

It took Harry a while to get to my house because of the roads. I was very nervous about riding with him on the icy roads, but I really was looking forward to seeing him. He opened the driver's side door and told me to hop in. I sat next to him as closely as possible. His brother, Jeremy, came with him.

When we finally made it to their house, Harry got out of the car and helped me out. We went inside and sat on the couch. We were watching, mostly listening, to MTV and kissing. I was really enjoying the music.

Jeremy said, "Want to check out Harry's new stereo? It is really cool!" I shrugged my shoulders and got up to follow him to Harry's bedroom. He was behind us.

Once we made it to the bedroom, Jeremy stepped out and closed the door. Harry grabbed me and started kissing me. He told me to lie down on the bed. I didn't want to. I turned and reached for the door. He grabbed me and pushed me down on the bed. I tried to fight him. I kicked and I screamed, but there was no one to save me.

After he was done, he said, "Well, let's get you home." I got dressed, and we went out to the car. I got into the back seat. It was a long, silent ride home. I cried all the way home.

When we finally made it to my house, I got out of the car and he drove away. I dried my tears as well as I could and went inside. Anna was in the kitchen. When I came in, she said, "Memaw knows you were gone, and she wants you to call her."

I picked up the phone and called her. "Where did you go?" she asked. I told her I went to my friend Ricki's. I said, "Please don't tell Mama." She said she wouldn't but that I had to. I told her I would and hung up the phone.

I went straight to the bathroom to take a shower. I just stood there with the water running over my face and cried. "How stupid! This is your fault!" I told myself. "Why didn't you just stay home?" I asked as I sat down in the shower and cried. "You deserved what you got for sneaking out."

I didn't tell Mama or Daddy what I had done or what happened. How could I? Daddy would be so mad. I decided to wait to tell. I couldn't even tell Anna. I told Memaw I was going to tell them when it was the right time.

CHAPTER NINETEEN

One week had passed before the snow and ice melted on the roads and we got to go back to school. At lunch break me, Ricki, my best friend at the time, and some other friends went to the store next to the school off campus.

Diego, a boy from school, was working the cash register. I asked for a pack of cigarettes for a friend, and he rang it up. He asked if I'd like a piece of Grape or Sour Apple Double bubble gum.

"Sure. I'll take a Grape piece."

He handed me the gum and asked, "Would you like to go out with me?"

I quickly replied, "No, thank you." Then I joined Ricki and the others in the back room.

On the way to school, I put the piece of gum in my mouth. As soon as I bit into it, I noticed it made my mouth numb and tasted different.

A short time later, I blacked out at my desk and fell onto the floor. I woke up to the teacher fanning me with a piece of paper. She asked if I was okay or if I needed to go to the nurse. I said I was fine. I really wasn't. The room was spinning, or was it my head? Something was definitely spinning. Something was not right. Soon I thought I was feeling better.

I was in the band, and we had practice after school. I was learning how to play the drums. Eugene was the guy teaching me. Since kindergarten, I had known him. He was very patient with me and had nice eyes. The snare drum was not working for me, so I switched to the baritone instead.

I liked playing the baritone. On the way to the football field for practice, I blacked out again. When I woke up, Eugene asked me if I was okay. "Yes," I said. We went on to the football field for our band practice.

That night my parents had some friends over for dinner. I was upstairs in my room when I began to feel funny. I went down to the dining room. Earlier that day the school nurse had called my house and told my parents about the incident and to keep an eye on me, so when Mama looked over, she asked if I was okay, and I replied, "No." I said that I felt weird. Then I blacked out.

When I woke up, they were taking me to the emergency room. The doctor ordered an MRI. Then I blacked out in front of the nurse. Daddy said when I woke up I was confused, so the doctor decided to keep me overnight.

Memaw came to visit the next day, and she asked if I had told Mama or Daddy what I had done. She thought the blackouts could be associated with the day I had snuck out. I assured her that wasn't the reason.

Nothing was reported in the MRI for a diagnosis, so the next day the doctor released me.

I wanted to go back to school the next day. I'm glad that I did because there were about ten other girls passing out like me and waking up confused. My daddy went to one of the girls' houses. Her name was Jenny, and he witnessed her blacking out, and it was exactly like my spells.

It was our halftime show at the football game. When I took a right face, it appeared to me that the band was an army with weapons and were after me. I remember running from them, but that was all I remembered.

Daddy was a sheriff's officer on duty that night and was the officer that found me. An elderly lady had called the police and said someone was hiding in her bushes with a big, shiny object.

He took me to the hospital, and I had a really bad blackout, where I was unconscious for forty-five minutes. I was admitted into the hospital. The doctor ordered a spinal tap this time. Daddy said when I came to that I didn't even know who he was. It broke his heart. He was scared for me and knew that I was really scared too.

The doctor came into my room. He said, "Well, I think we finally have some answers."

Daddy asked, "Is it good or bad?"

The doctor replied, "The good news is hopefully in a matter of time they will stop on their own. The bad news is your daughter has tested positive for both PCP and LSD."

I screamed loudly, "But I have never done any kind of drugs, Daddy, I promise!" I began to cry hysterically.

The doctor said, "I believe that is true. These levels are dangerously high."

Daddy was stunned. "How could this happen?" he asked.

"Sir, I believe she was drugged. Now we need to find out how these drugs are being administered to her."

Daddy asked me if I had eaten something someone had given me. He believed me since ten other girls had these same symptoms. This was a bigger issue than he first thought.

He started by trying to figure out what all that we had in common was. I confessed to Daddy that I smoked cigarettes. I had a pack in my purse that we'd picked up at the band hall. He carefully looked at a few of the cigarettes and noticed the ones along the outside of the pack all had black dots on them. He held the pack up to the light and saw tiny holes all throughout the pack.

"I think someone is injecting the cigarettes. I am going to take these to the lab at the sheriff's office. Do the girls you know having the spells smoke too?"

I knew they did, so I nodded.

"Where do you buy them?" he asked.

"At the store next to the school. I think Diego did it," I replied.

"Who's Diego?" he asked me.

"He works at the store and goes to school with us. He asked me out, and I said no. I heard him ask Jenny out too. She also said no."

Daddy felt sure that me, Jenny, and the other girls had been drugged by Diego. He took the cigarettes to the lab to be tested and asked the technician if he could get a rush on the results.

Mama came to the hospital, and Daddy was at the sheriff's office waiting for results. He had called the girls he knew to be blacking out and asked if they smoked and if Diego had asked them out. Five of the girls had answered yes. The lab technician radioed Daddy. He had the results. The cigarettes had tested positive.

The sheriff's office got a warrant. They had a task team put together. First, one of the officers called the store. The owner told him that Diego was off.

They surrounded his house. They knocked on the door and announced their presence. When no one answered, they busted their way in. Diego was in the bedroom with a gun. He was warned to put it down, which he refused. He was then shot after he pointed it at an officer.

It didn't go the way we all wanted it to, but at least he would not be in the streets hurting any more girls. We were lucky one of us hadn't died of an overdose.

Finally, I got to go home, and the blackouts came further apart until they didn't come anymore. I quit smoking cigarettes too, and I didn't leave campus anymore at lunch.

CHAPTER TWENTY

The following school year I was more supervised. I did get to go to Ricki's some. I called her mom Moma T. I just loved her. She always treated me like one of the family. When we would stay at Ricki's rather than my house, we would go on newspaper routes with Moma T. Wes, a friend from school, and Donnie, Ricki's boyfriend, would go with us.

Wes eventually admitted he liked me and wanted me to be his girlfriend. I thought that was wonderful, so I agreed. He was really sweet. He would come to my house and go to church with us or just come over to hang out and eat dinner. Daddy really liked him a lot.

Wes and his brother, Paul, came to Mamaw's house and put wooden panels on her living room ceiling. They did a really great job, and Mamaw and Aunt Elsa wanted to pay them, but they wouldn't accept it.

They both just said they had heard she cooked and would be happy with a home-cooked meal. I suggested to Mamaw that she bake one of her homemade chocolate pies too.

So Mamaw got to cooking some ham, mashed potatoes, fried squash, cornbread, and green beans. For dessert, she made that homemade chocolate pie. She even made a picture of her delicious sweet tea.

There was a pool table upstairs. Wes, Paul, Anna, and I went up there to play for a while. I was glad that Mamaw, Daddy, and Elsa really liked Wes. I liked him a lot.

Wes never forced me to do anything like J.R. or Harry had. That made me feel good. I really felt like I could trust him.

I got up early every school morning to ride to the elementary school where Memaw worked, so I could ride the bus with Wes. He just lived across the street. Cold mornings were especially nice because it was warm snuggled in his arms.

Wes and I saw each other for a while. Then one day as we walked hand in hand, as we always did, he let go as we got to the front door of the school. He said, "There's my mom. Let me see what she is doing here." He gave me a quick kiss and went to talk to her. She lived in Kentucky, so it was strange that she was here.

In class it was hard to stay focused on what the teacher was saying. I kept looking at my watch and classroom clock. Once class was over, Ricki met me in the hall. She had a note that Wes had written to me. She said, "I'm not supposed to give it to you until school is out, but I thought you deserved to see it now."

In Wes's note, it said that he was sorry, he didn't know how to tell me, but he was moving to his mom's for a while. What? How could he do this to me? My heart crumbled as I crumbled the note. I just couldn't believe what I had read. I read it again and again. It still didn't make sense. We had just started saying "I love you" to each other. I gave him my heart, and he shredded it.

CHAPTER TWENTY-ONE

I was in a deep depression. Everything was hitting me at the same time. There was my mama, who wasn't mine—my real one was dead; the molestation; the rape; the being drugged; and now Wes just left me without a proper goodbye. I felt worthless, like I had no reason to go on living.

I told Daddy that I wanted to kill myself, that I didn't deserve to live. He went into the other room and came back with his gun. He tried to give it to me, but I wouldn't take it.

"That's not how I want to die!" I screamed.

He pointed the gun to my head and said, "Want me to do it for you?"

I bursted into tears, asking, "No! Why? Are you going to shoot me?"

He then said, "No, because you really don't want to die. Let's get you some help." Daddy took me to the hospital and told the nurse, "My daughter needs help. She is suicidal."

I just sat in the waiting area crying until someone came up to me. It was a lady with kind eyes. She asked me to come with her, so I stood up and followed her. My legs trembled as I walked.

We came to a door where she had to use a card to open it. Once through the doorway, the door slammed loudly. We went to a room with a bunch of tables and chairs. She asked that I sit down with Daddy. It was there my daddy began to sign a lot of paperwork.

Once he was done with the paperwork, she asked me to come with her. We went to a room, much like a hospital room, and she said, "This bed by the window will be yours. You'll need to give me your shoelaces."

Next she asked me if I had anything in my pockets. When I said no, she told me to take off my clothes and put these scrubs on. She waited there while I did that, and she told me I could put my clothes in this bag she handed me.

She introduced me to Sharon, my roommate, and asked her to show me around and introduce me to other patients. Sharon showed me the TV room, the music room, the dining room, and the nurse station. She also introduced me to some of the patients.

A tall cart came into the hallway with a plastic-zipped cover.

Sharon said, "That's dinner. Don't worry, the food is pretty good here." Another lady passing by agreed with her.

At dinner I met some of the other patients. There were a few of different age groups. One of the cute teen guys caught my eye.

I asked Sharon, "Who's the blond-headed guy?"

She answered, "That is Heath. He is really sweet."

I laughed and said, "And really cute." She laughed back.

I noticed at dinner he kept looking over at me. I finally got up the nerve to go talk to him.

"Hi! I am Daisy."

He replied, "Hi! I am Heath. It is really nice to meet you, Daisy. Would you like to go listen to some music in the music room?"

I answered, "Sure, that sounds nice."

We listened to some Aerosmith, Kiss, Whitesnake, and Eagles. Just got to know a little about each other. Talked a lot about religion. We both were Christians, but struggling with why things were happening to us the way they were.

Going to group was helpful. At least I knew I wasn't alone with my feelings. I felt I had been cursed or punished for something but unsure of what that was. The group leader wanted us to write a play about who had hurt us the worst and what we would say to them. I had a problem with this exercise. I felt I had been hurt equally by several people.

Where it got interesting was in the one-on-one sessions. I felt comfortable here. I could tell the psychologist whatever I wanted under client-doctor privilege, and she couldn't tell. So I told her everything from the abuse I received from J.R., what Harry had done to me, and having to deal with what Diego did on top of it all. It was just too much.

I had just learned that J.R. had been discharged from the army and was home with his wife. My counselor thought it would be good to set up a session with him and my dad. That way I could work through it. I agreed to it.

The next day I was called into her office. When I came in, Daddy and J.R. were there. I wanted to walk out until the counselor told me that she hadn't told them why they were there, just that they needed to hear me out.

I looked at Daddy, not J.R.

The counselor said, "Daisy, tell your father and brother why they are here today."

I looked at her and began to cry as I told Daddy what happened to me the day I had snuck out with Harry. "It was my fault it happened. If I wouldn't have left, then it would not have happened."

This really upset J.R.. He stood up and asked where he could find him. I looked at J.R. with hatred in my eyes and told Daddy loudly what he had also done to me and that he told me that I was the reason our mother was killed.

J.R. said he only did what he did one time to me and that I was confusing it with what Harry had done, making up what he had said. The counselor asked J.R. to step out. Then she said, "Daisy is deeply affected by these things she claims J.R. has done." She paused. "I don't believe that these events are imagined."

Daddy just sat there in a distant stare. Like he was in shock.

"I think J.R. needs to return to the room and apologize to Daisy for what he has done. It impacted her not only physically but emotionally too." She got up and walked out to give Daddy and me a moment alone.

"You don't believe me, do you, Daddy? I promise I am not making up or imagining what J.R. said. He told me it was my fault our mama had died. Do you hate me too?" I asked him. "I am so depressed and feel so alone. I want to die. At least then all the bad things will stop happening to me."

I told Daddy I had started smoking cigarettes again since I was so stressed out, but I always checked for pin holes and black marks on the cigarettes. I couldn't believe it, but he left me some cigarettes of his own, said he would go to the store and bring me some more too. He gave me a big, tight hug, and he and J.R. left.

I felt better since I had gotten a few things off my chest. I went to the phone to call Memaw and tell her that I had told Daddy about the day I had snuck out. She was relieved. She asked me to please not do that again.

She also asked, "Can you promise me something?"

"What's that?" I asked her.

She answered, "Promise me that you won't get pregnant?"

I shrugged my shoulders, which she could not see, and said, "I won't."

CHAPTER TWENTY-TWO

Four weeks had gone by, and I was finally released. I called Ricki to tell her that I was home. I thought she would be happy to hear from me.

She asked, "You know that Wes is back, don't you?"

My heart dropped as I replied, "No, I didn't know that." He hadn't tried to reach me while I was in the hospital. I couldn't afford for him to hurt me again because I was so vulnerable. It would be best if I just didn't see him. I asked Ricki to come spend a couple of days with me. She did, and I was so glad. I needed my friend, especially my best friend.

When she got to the house, I ran out and gave her a big hug. She said, "If you ever try that again, I will kill you first."

I replied to her, "Thank you for being my friend, I won't do it again."

The next couple of days, Ricki and I spent a lot of time outside. We rode horses, bicycles, went fishing, and occasionally just laid out in the sun.

Wes was one of the first people I saw when I got back to school. He tried to talk to me, but I just walked away. I wasn't taking a chance on giving him another one.

I saw Eugene walk into the band hall, so I went in there. The Sadie Hawkins Dance was coming up, so I thought I would ask him to go.

When I walked in, he was standing on the band director's platform. I went up to him.

"Eugene, can I ask you something?" I asked.

"Sure," he replied.

"Will you go to the Sadie Hawkins Dance with me?"

He replied, "No, I'm not into those kind of things." I could not get out of the band hall fast enough, tears in my eyes.

I ran into Ricki and went into the bathroom. She followed and asked, "What is wrong, Daisy? Did Wes do something?"

I washed my face off and answered, "No. It was Eugene. I asked him to go to the Sadie Hawkins Dance with me, and he said no."

Ricki shook her and grabbed my arm. "Come on, let's get you out of this nasty bathroom. You know, he's missing out, right?"

I laughed and said, "You always know exactly what to say." We went to class.

I ran into Wes at lunch. It was only a matter of time that I would be forced to speak to him again. I guess today was that day. He came over to me and Ricki and asked if he could speak to me.

Ricki quickly said, "I don't think so."

I told her it was okay. "Let me see what he wants."

"Thank you," he said. "I wanted to know if we can start over again and be friends?"

I just stared at him. "You mean to say after you were supposedly in love with me and ran off like you did, you want to know if we can be friends?" I huffed. "Let me think about it. You hurt me badly. I thought I could trust you, and you said nothing to me and just left. How am I supposed to get over that?" I asked him. I started to walk away and yelled for Ricki to come with me. She came along with me, and we went to the hallway before class began.

"What did he want?" she asked.

I replied, "For me to give him another chance to be friends. You know it will be only a matter of time before he'll want to be more. I think I should tell him that I really don't want to take a chance on him hurting me again. It took me so long to get past that." Ricki agreed.

Walking down the school hall, Ricki whispered, "Daisy, I have something I need to tell you." She sounded serious.

"What is it?" I asked her.

"I just found out this morning that I am pregnant."

I was shocked. "Does Mama T. know?" I asked her.

"Yes. Donnie and I are getting married next weekend."

I thought I was going to faint. "Seriously?"

She responded, "It will be just a small ceremony with our parents as witnesses."

Again, I was really shocked.

"I won't be finishing school, and we are moving."

I was going to lose my best friend.

CHAPTER TWENTY-THREE

Anna had the same best friend since they had been in third grade. Her name was Autumn. I would take Anna to Autumn's house to spend the night or pick Autumn up for sleepovers at our house. She had the best-looking brother named Dean Jr.. I would walk Anna in just with hopes I would see him. A few times he was home, and his mom, Beth, would point to his room.

Prom was coming up, and I was trying to build up the courage to ask Dean Jr. to go with me. We had talked on the phone several times for hours at a time or visited when I went over there for Anna.

I finally decided I was going to ask Dean Jr. to the prom. He called me one afternoon after school, and we talked for a bit. The conversation was going well.

"So, Dean, will you go to the prom with me?" I asked. There was only silence. I asked, "Are you still there?"

Finally, he responded, "Well, someone else already asked me. I don't want to hurt anybody's feelings. I think I'll just go to the after-party."

I didn't want this to make things awkward between us, and he assured me it wouldn't and we'd still be good friends.

"Great! Because I really like talking to you."

He said, "I like talking to you too."

We said bye and hung up the phone.

There was this sweet girl, Kim, in my English class. She and her boyfriend, Brian, had gone out for most of high school. I asked her if they were going to the prom.

She said, "Of course we are," and asked me, "Are you going?"

I told her I had asked Dean Jr., but he had turned me down, and I did not have a date.

"Brian has a younger brother. I'd bet he would go with you," she said.

I knew Tim from school. He was nice, so I told her to go ahead and ask him for me.

The next day she came to class and said, "Tim said he would go with you."

I asked her, "You did tell him this was as friends only, right?" She said she had. I just did not want to give him the wrong impression. I had no feelings for him whatsoever.

It was the night of the prom. I had a black strapless formal dress. It was long in the back and shorter in the front, turquoise netting underneath along with a turquoise bow at my right hip. Memaw had made it from my design.

Mama, Daddy, and I met Kim, her parents, her date, Brian, and Tim at a restaurant in town. We all looked sharp. After dinner, a lot of pictures were taken, and the four of us were off to the prom.

After we all had our prom pictures taken, Kim asked me, "Do you and Tim want to go with us? We rented a hotel room in town." They were my ride, so I agreed.

The first person I ran into there was Dean Jr. He told me how beautiful I looked and said we could see each other later. I hoped so.

I went to a room with some other people I knew from school. They had the bathtub full of iced-down alcoholic drinks and told me to help myself. So I had one of them. My daddy told me to be home by midnight, so I kept a close eye on the time.

I saw Dean again and told him I had to go home but hoped we could talk later.

"Of course," he said. "You be careful going home."

When I got home, I was sure to hold my breath as Mama let me in. I went straight to my room, changed my clothes, and got into bed. There I lay as I thought of Dean Jr. until I was fast asleep.

CHAPTER TWENTY-FOUR

It was a week before my seventeenth birthday. I was so sick that I could not even hold down water. No meds were helping either. Mama took me to the ER fearing that I was dehydrated. The doctor had ordered some lab work.

An hour or so had gone by when he came into the room. Mama had stepped out a moment.

The doctor said, "You are not sick. I am afraid to say, you are pregnant." I was stunned. "Since you are a minor, I will have to tell your mom. Would you like me to do that here or out in the hall?" he asked.

"The hall please," I answered as Mama came back into the room.

He asked her to step out with him. I heard her scream loudly, "No!" She was wiping tears away as she came back into the room.

"I'm sorry," I said to her.

She asked, "Who is the father?"

I looked down and said, "Dean Jr., Autumn's brother." The doctor gave me something for nausea and sent me home.

When we made it home, Daddy wasn't home yet. He made it home just as we stepped in. He came up to me and kissed me on the forehead and asked, "Are you feeling better?"

I answered, "Daddy, please don't be mad. I am not sick."

He asked, "Then what is wrong?" as he took his gun holster off.

I said, "I am pregnant."

He then threw his holster with guns inside into the living room. "Who is the father?" he demanded.

"It is Autumn's brother, Dean Jr."

He was so mad. He threatened to hurt him. My daddy didn't speak to me for two weeks.

Dean Jr. had been staying with Toby. I went over there to tell Dean the news in person. Toby answered the door when I knocked. I asked him if I could speak to Dean. He told me it wasn't a good time, that he was asleep.

"Look, Toby, I am pregnant. I need to tell him."

He said, "Oh, okay," as he showed me the room he was in.

I knocked on the bedroom door and announced my presence as I entered. "Dean, we need to talk," I said.

He sat up and gave me a kiss. "What's wrong?" he asked.

"I am pregnant."

"What? What are your parents going to say?" he asked.

I told him how I had found out and that they already knew. He felt my belly and said, "You are already showing a little."

I agreed as I told him that my dad wanted to have a meeting with him. I had to go home, but he agreed to meet with my dad. I asked him to call me later as I left.

A few days later, Dean came over to the house and met my dad. He told Dean that he expected his help with doctor bills. Dean agreed to do his best.

I didn't know it, but instead of Dean sending my dad the money, it was his mother, Beth. Anna had told Autumn about the pregnancy, so she told Beth. It wasn't that she didn't like me, but she felt I was too young and would end up pregnant.

I had an ultrasound that confirmed my feelings. It was a girl. Aunt Elsa managed a maternity store and bought me so many cute maternity clothes. She and Mama had a baby shower for me at Mamaw's. I got so many beautiful dresses and things that would be especially useful when she was born.

Dean had been avoiding me and going around telling everyone the baby was not his. That broke my heart. I was now six months pregnant and may have only seen him three times since I found out.

How could he deny this baby? I was so depressed throughout the pregnancy. I felt being pregnant gave me permission to eat what and when I wanted to. I gained over eighty pounds.

I asked God to forgive me of my sins, to keep this baby safe and healthy, and to allow Dean to want to be there for his child. I needed the

Lord to guide me. I really messed up and was deeply sorry. The actions I had taken were not very Christian-like, and I felt awfully bad that I had sinned in this way.

I got a call from Wes. He was joining the army and wanted to ask me one more time to take him back, that he loved me and always would. I told him no, and I really wanted to try to make it work with Dean once I had the baby. He was sad as he told me he knew that I always had a thing for Dean. I didn't see him before he left for basic training.

Feeling my baby doing what I felt were somersaults in my belly made me sad that there was no one special to share it with besides Anna. She loved to feel her kicking and would talk to her. She couldn't wait to be an aunt.

Since Anna and Autumn were best friends, they thought it was so awesome that they were going to share a niece. Dean's older sister, Leena, had said that she was babysitting when I went back to school. She already was at the house babysitting their younger brother, Aaron.

Aaron was only four. He would hide in a closet or under a bed when I came over, scared I would get him pregnant. I thought that was the funniest thing. When he had asked Leena how I had gotten pregnant, she had told him by kissing. So he thought if I kissed him, he would get pregnant.

It was early February, and I was having pains. When I told Mama, she said we should time them. They were coming every ten minutes or so. I was scared. Since I found out that I was pregnant, I had also been talking to Ricki since she had been through it recently.

When the pains came every five minutes, we went to Mamaw's. After all, she just lived across the street from the hospital.

The baby was not due for a couple of more weeks. I was getting scared. I called Ricki and another girl, Dana, I had gotten close to in school and let them know we were about to go to the hospital.

Anna called Autumn to let her family know. Dean was home, but they didn't even tell him before they left.

The doctor came into my room and said that he was going to have to break my water because it hadn't done so on its own. This was when I really got scared. It was happening.

So many people were here waiting for the arrival of my baby. They were eager to meet her. Except for her father that is.

I told my friend Dana to call Dean to tell him that I was in labor. This would be the last chance for him to be a part of the baby's life. He told her that he didn't have a ride, so she offered to go pick him up. He agreed, so she left the hospital to go get him.

The anesthesiologist came in to give me an epidural. I asked him if my mama could stay in the room with me.

He answered, "Was your mom in the room with you when you got pregnant? I think if you were a big enough girl to get pregnant, you can handle it."

Wow! How hateful, I thought.

Beth took Autumn and Anna to her house so they could go to sleep for a while. Daddy made Mamaw go home. All that was left at the hospital were Mama, Daddy, Ricki, Dana, and Dean.

Dean asked Ricki if she wanted to go for a walk with him. She agreed to go. I knew as soon as they left the room that I would be wheeled into delivery.

Seemed like they had just left the room, the nurse checked me, and I was ready to go to the delivery room. How would Dean and Ricki find me? Dana said she would stay behind and let them know where I had gone.

I had Mama go to the delivery room with me. She held my hand as I pushed. I squeezed her hand tightly as I pushed. Just a few pushes and the nurse laid a baby girl on my belly.

She was so heavy, I thought. Then the nurse took her and cleaned her up. They put her on the scale, and Mama held her fingers up to let everyone know how much she weighed. "Eight pounds, one ounce," born at 1:21 AM.

Dean called his mother to let her know. She was so excited. She woke Anna and Autumn to let them know they were now aunts. Lacy had been born!

After I was taken to a room and got settled in, Dean came in. He asked, "Can you see if they can bring in the baby?" I called the nursery and asked the nurse to bring her to the room.

When they brought her in, Dean quickly scooped her up into his arms.

I said, "Her name is Lacy Renay. Do you like it?"

He answered, "Yes, it's very pretty."

I asked, "You want her to have your last name?" I was so happy when he said yes.

That afternoon, Beth brought Anna and Autumn up to see her granddaughter and their niece. They were all so excited to see her and get to love on her. I had the prettiest little dress for her hospital pictures to be taken in and wear when we got to go home.

Daddy came to visit her too. I saw how proud of her he was when he held her. There were no grudges against me anymore, just love. He tried to get me to go ahead and have Lacy released from the hospital because she was healthy and could go home. I had some post-birth difficulties and had to stay in the hospital longer than normal new moms do. I told him she should stay with me since I was trying to breastfeed.

Dean didn't leave the hospital for two days. The only reason he left that day was because he had to go to court. I was scared when he didn't come back to the hospital. I found out later that he had just gone home to get some rest. He had been placed on probation by the court.

Beth and Leena came up every day to see Lacy. They were so in love with her, and it was Beth's first granddaughter and Leena's first niece. Even Aaron loved her when he came to visit.

Finally, after a week, Lacy and I got to go home. The crib was set up in the guest room, so that was where Lacy and I would sleep. I was happy not to have to climb all the stairs to go to my room.

CHAPTER TWENTY-FIVE

Lacy was six weeks old, and I had to stop breastfeeding. My milk had dried up. Poor baby, I had been starving her. I put her on formula, and she slept through the night for the first time ever. I was so excited! I still woke up a couple of times during the night to make sure that she was still breathing.

I was getting ready to go back to school soon instead of home school, and I wanted to get Lacy familiar with Leena because she would be babysitting her while I was in school. So I took her over to Dean's house as much as possible.

I asked Daddy if it was okay for me to move into Dean's parents' house.

He said, "You are an adult, so you can make your own decisions."

I told Beth, "Thank you so much for allowing us to stay here."

She showed me where I would be sleeping. She also insisted since Lacy was sleeping all night that she just kept the crib in her room. I could still put her to bed.

I began to unpack and get settled in. I was going to be starting school tomorrow and was very nervous. Leena was excited to have her baby five days a week while I was in school.

I felt it would really work out since I had late arrival for school. It would give me the chance to get Lacy dressed and fed before I left for school. Leena arrived early anyway so she could watch Aaron. He wasn't old enough to go to school yet. He told Leena he was going to be Lacy's babysitter. She thought that was cute.

It was my first morning at Dean's. I got up and was going to check on Lacy. Leena already had her and was feeding her.

I said, "Oh, I'm sorry. I meant to be up to get her as she woke up."

Leena replied, "Well, her aunt Leena beat you to it." I went ahead and got dressed for school.

I went home at lunch to check on Lacy. Most days Dean was still asleep. Some days he was awake and would visit with me while I ate lunch.

Dean and I had been talking about getting married. He said, "As soon as you finish school, we will set a date."

My dad had given me my mom's wedding ring, so I started wearing the engagement ring.

I had fallen behind in school and didn't see a way I would be able to graduate with my class, so I enrolled into an alternative school. I would receive a diploma from the school I was set to originally graduate from. They also had a day care that Lacy could go to while I was in school.

One Saturday, Lacy and I were home alone, and I was folding and putting clothes away. I walked by her playpen where she had been napping. She was blue. I quickly pulled her out of the playpen, lay her on the floor, and covered her nose and mouth with my mouth, blowing breaths in.

Finally, she began to cough. I picked her up, and she was like a rag doll. I went to the kitchen and called 911. My dad was at work and heard the call come in. He beat the ambulance there. He was so upset to see Lacy as lethargic as she was. Being a firefighter, he radioed for the ambulance to get here as quickly as they could.

When we got to the hospital, I called Dean. He was quick to get there. Once the doctor came in, he let us know that he wanted Lacy to go to the children's hospital. It was about two hours away.

They took her by ambulance, and I rode with Lacy. Dean followed in the car. Daddy told us to keep him posted. They would come if needed after Lacy was checked out.

I prayed the whole ambulance ride to God. I apologized and asked him to forgive me for my sins, and I prayed for Lacy to be okay and for his guidance.

A few tests were done before the doctor came in and told us that the epiglottis was too small to completely close and milk was going into her airway. They were going to give her Reglan, and if it didn't help, she would require surgery.

Lacy spent the night and was observed with medication for any side effects. There weren't any, so they released her.

I stayed home with her for a week just to be sure that she was okay.

Then we went back to school. The day care workers had missed her and were happy to have her back.

When graduation day finally came, Lacy got to have a graduation from day care as well. When I took her to the stage to get her diploma, she showed off by waving to everyone and saying hi. I was glad Daddy got it on video.

There were only five of us that graduated that day. With it being a small group, we all had to give a speech. I was so nervous. In mine I thanked my supporters, including my parents, my extended family, friends, the administration of the alternative school, and the day care staff.

After all the setbacks, I had graduated from high school. It was something that my daddy doubted would happen since I had quit school just six weeks prior to graduation from the original high school. I would not have quit had I not been so far behind. There was just no way I could have caught up to do so. It was November, but I had graduated.

Now that I had graduated, Dean and I had to pick a date for our wedding. He told me when we got home that night we would grab a calendar and pick a date. I couldn't wait to make our little family official!

Right after we had picked out the date, Leena gave birth to a healthy baby boy. Now Lacy had a cousin to play with, and Dean and I had a nephew. His name was William, and he was just too cute.

CHAPTER TWENTY-SIX

It was a few weeks before the wedding, and I was feeling sick. I took a pregnancy test, and it came back positive. Dean and I decided not to tell anyone until after the wedding since it was so close.

The wedding was going to be at my parents' house. The ring bearer–best man would be Aaron. The flower girls would be Dean's little cousin, Noel and Lacy. My daddy would give me away.

It was September 25, the night before the wedding. I stayed at my parents' house so Mama could help me get dressed. She was going to take me to Aunt Vickie's hair studio so she could fix my hair. Mama was going to do my makeup and nails.

We were almost ready. Aunt Vickie was putting Lacy's hair up and the final touches on her flower basket. Noel looked beautiful in her little pink ruffle dress too.

Everyone was here except Dean and his father. The ceremony was to start at two o'clock in the afternoon. It was ten minutes after, and there was no sign of them. I began to cry thinking he was standing me up. I was hormonal too, but no one knew that.

Aaron came to my parents' room, looking handsome in his little tuxedo, to tell us they had arrived. I had my cousin, Timmy, light the candles. Aaron went down the hallway first with his little pillow. Next Noel went with Lacy. I heard Lacy shout "Fire! Fire!" as she saw the candles entering the living room. Everyone was laughing and saying "Aw!"

Now it was my turn. My stomach was a ball of nerves. I entered the living room with my daddy by my side, and everyone stood up and looked at me. I looked over at Dean. He was all smiles and looking handsome in his tuxedo as well.

The pastor, Brother Jim, from our church was the officiant. We had attended a premarital class with him prior to the wedding. Mine and Dean's eyes locked and we never looked anywhere but each other. I don't even remember saying vows. I just remember Brother Jim saying, "I now pronounce you husband and wife. You may kiss the bride."

Next we went into the kitchen for cake and punch. Dean and I gave each other a bite of cake. He was so gentle and didn't smash it into my face as I had imagined him doing. We gave each other a drink of punch. Then we visited with everyone as we received congratulations.

We went into the guest room and changed our clothes so we could leave and enjoy some time alone as husband and wife. Lacy was going to stay with my parents. Dean's mom had gotten a nice suite for us at a hotel in town, along with a bottle of wine. Neither one of us were old enough to purchase alcohol yet. I was only nineteen, and he was twenty.

After a little alone time at the suite, we decided to go to the fair that was in town. It was nice running into friends and announcing that we had just gotten married. Everyone was congratulating us.

In the meantime, we were just going to enjoy our alone time as newlyweds. So we went to pick up a pizza, which ended up on the house as a wedding gift, and went back to the hotel.

I was so tired. After all, it had been a very long day. I was too excited to sleep the night before. Not long after I lay my head down, I was fast asleep.

CHAPTER TWENTY-SEVEN

It was the first of October, and our apartment was finally ready. Dean and I were packing up his and my dad's trucks with all our stuff.

Living room furniture we had picked out was being delivered. I couldn't believe that we were moving into our first place as a little family. Lacy had never slept in a room alone, so this would be interesting.

We got everything unpacked and even all the home decor up on the walls and on the tables. My dad had given us a big console TV where our wedding pictures sat on.

Dean tried to put Lacy in her bed in her new room, but she was not having it. His mom had told us if it didn't work, to put her toddler bed in our room and move it closer to her room every night. We started night 1 right next to our bed. Here she was fine and went straight to sleep.

The next morning I was going to have my first doctor visit at the OBGYN. We still hadn't told anyone yet. We were waiting until we were married and in our own place.

The doctor said I was about six weeks along. He would do a sonogram at my next month's visit. We decided to wait a couple of more weeks to tell our families. Keeping this a secret was hard. I wanted to tell everyone.

I went to work up the road at the pizza restaurant, and Dean was a bingo caller at the local bingo hall. All the older ladies loved it when he called out the numbers from the balls. I didn't like it so much because on the weekends he worked until four o'clock in the morning.

A couple of weeks went by, and we decided it was okay to tell that we were expecting again. It didn't go as bad as I thought it would. Everyone said they figured it was just a matter of time.

We had been able to get Lacy's bed in the hallway, so we were making progress. She loved hanging out in her room playing during the day. Sometimes she would even fall asleep in there as she played.

On the weekends either Anna or Autumn would come stay with me. Sometimes they both would. We would have fun movie or game nights. They were excited they were going to be aunts again soon.

On the weekday nights, Dean would get off at eleven at night, but I noticed he was not coming straight home. Sometimes he wouldn't come home at all. We started fighting a lot. I didn't like that some fights were in front of Lacy.

I felt like he was cheating on me. I was only working part-time because I had Lacy at home, and either his mom or my parents would get her on their days off so I could work. I was probably more stressed than I should be considering I was pregnant.

When it came time for my next appointment, Mama came to get me and go with me. Dean had to work, and Leena had Lacy.

I couldn't wait to see the baby on the sonogram. The lab tech started moving the transducer around, taking some measurements. Then she said she needed to get the doctor and would be right back.

I looked at Mama and started to cry. What could be wrong? Why did she need to get the doctor?

Mama just rubbed my shoulder and said, "Stay calm. It may not be anything. The doctor will be in, and we will see. Take deep breaths and relax."

The doctor came in and looked at my belly some more. Then he asked, "Do twins run in your family?"

I looked at him in shock and answered, "Not that I know of. Why do you ask?" His answer was, "Well, you are expecting twins. See here is baby number 1 and here is baby number 2."

I immediately started crying. "How are we going to take care of three kids? What is Dean going to say?" So many thoughts raced through my head.

Mama took me home after the appointment. I had called Dean and told him to come straight home. I lay on the couch talking to Mama. "This doesn't seem real." I had the sonogram picture in my hand to prove it though.

At four-thirty Dean came home on his break. "What's wrong?" he asked. I sat up on the couch and told him to sit down. I just started crying and handed him the picture. "Twins?" he asked.

"Yes," I cried.

"It'll be okay," he said. "We'll make it work. Maybe they'll be boys." He smiled. "We can handle three kids right now."

I said, "We have plenty of help. It will be okay."

He couldn't wait to get back to work to tell everyone. I got the privilege of calling his family to tell them. His mom took it better than I thought she would. Leena was super-excited and said she would quit her job to help us out. She promised not to tell Lacy. Dean and I wanted to. She brought Lacy home. She and I baked cookies and watched *Barney*. She loved *Barney*, and we always had to have it on the TV, or she would throw a fit. I kept her awake until Dean got home from work so we could tell her.

He came in the door, and I heard her scream "Daddy!" from the kitchen. When I came into the living room, he was spinning her around. I told them to sit down.

"Lacy, Daddy and I need to talk to you."

Dean held her close and said, "Mommy has two babies growing in her belly."

I added, "You are going to be their big sister."

She laughed and said, "They are going to have to mind me." We couldn't help but laugh.

I looked at them as I thought, *We are going from three to five. How are we going to manage that? It will be a big change.* About that time, I felt butterflies in my belly. I told Dean, "I think I just felt them move." Our little family was going to grow quickly.

As we lay in bed that night, I felt them more. I guess there being two of them I could feel them sooner. I was only about thirteen weeks along according to the sonogram. Dean tried to feel them but couldn't. I didn't think they would be still enough for me to go to sleep. It was just little flutters, but they were constant.

I woke up to Lacy standing at the bedside with her hand on my belly. She was saying, "When y'all come out, you are not going to be crying all night keeping me awake. Mommy and I need our sleep." I just lay there with my eyes closed listening to her telling them how it was going to be.

CHAPTER TWENTY-EIGHT

I woke up in the middle of the night and shook Dean awake.

"Something is wrong," I said.

"It's just the trash truck," he said. "Go back to sleep."

I said, "No, something is wrong with the babies."

I got up to go to the bathroom and felt a gush. I turned on the light and saw that I was standing in a puddle of blood. I froze in place. Dean said, "Go to the bathroom." Then a trail of blood followed me.

Our phone had just been disconnected, and the car was in the shop. Lacy woke up to me crying and saw the trail of blood and started crying too. It was four-thirty in the morning.

Dean went running around the block until he saw a man awake in his kitchen. Banged on his door and asked to use his phone. He called an ambulance and ran back home to me. It seemed like forever until they finally arrived. It was too soon for the babies to be born. I was scared, and there was so much blood. The paramedics let Dean and Lacy ride to the hospital with us.

I prayed again to God and asked him if I was being punished for getting offtrack. Did I not want the babies enough? I apologized and told him that I did want them and that I loved them. I asked for forgiveness of all my sins and to light the path for me to follow.

The doctor came in and said he was going to admit me. I needed complete bed rest, and he diagnosed me with placenta previa. Nurses came in every two hours to listen for babies' heartbeats and take my blood pressure.

Lacy alternated between mine and Dean's parents and stayed with

Dean on his days off. They brought her to see me as much as possible. I missed her so much. I missed being home.

Even though I was bedridden, I was still bleeding. I was on high doses of iron because I had lost so much blood. I was tired of being stuck in bed. I couldn't even get up to use the bathroom. I had to use a bedpan. At least I had TV, which we didn't have at home.

Daddy came to see me every day when he was off. Since the hospital was across the street from her house, Mamaw and Aunt Elsa came to visit when they had off too and always brought me a nice meal.

If it weren't for visitors and TV, I didn't know what I would do besides be constantly bored. I enjoyed Lacy's visits. I missed her so much. Either Dean would bring her or his or my mom. She missed me too. I was always sad when she left.

Finally, after two straight weeks of being in the hospital, I may get to go home. It was Good Friday, April 9, 1992, and the doctor said if I continued to do as well as I was, that I could go home on Easter Sunday.

Everyone was so happy. We were beginning to think I was going to spend the duration of my pregnancy here. I was only six and a half months along. So that would really be a long time. Luckily, the bleeding had stopped, and that was why I could go home.

I woke up in the middle of the night when I felt a gush. I called the nurse in to change my bed pad. *Great!* I thought. *There goes my ticket for a release.*

At four-thirty Sunday morning, I called the nurse. I felt a lot of pressure. When the nurse checked me, she said I was crowning and needed to go to the delivery room. I had to call Dean. He was at work.

When I called and told him I was in labor, he hung up the phone. Before the nurse rolled me into delivery, Dean had made it and was in the hallway. The doctor told him to wait in the waiting room.

I only had to push twice, and the stillborn baby boy was born. The nurse cleaned him up a little and asked if I wanted to hold him. Of course I did. She went to get Dean. The baby was swaddled in a blue towel. I held him in my arms as I looked him over. Besides being as small as my hand, he looked perfect.

Dean came in, and I asked him if he wanted to hold him. At first he said no, but he changed his mind. I handed him over. The nurse said we should give him a name. We named him Devin Wade. I could still hear the second baby's heartbeat on the monitor and feel him moving around.

The doctor came in and said they would have to take the second baby because I had developed a severe infection. I broke down in tears, and so did Dean.

They put something in my IV, and I was going to sleep as they pushed me down the hall. When I woke up, I asked the nurse if the baby made it. She told me that his heart stopped beating right before the surgery. Then she handed me a card with both babies' footprints on it. We named the second one Kevin Dean. We donated both babies to pathology.

Monday, April 12, I got discharged from the hospital. It was sad going home empty-handed and not feeling their movements anymore.

CHAPTER TWENTY-NINE

It was two weeks after I lost the babies. I was running a 102-degree temperature. We still didn't have a phone. I took Lacy and we went next door to use the neighbor's phone. I called my dad to see if he would come take me to the hospital.

He took me to the ER. The doctor finally came in to see me. After an examination, he ordered some lab work. We had to wait for the results.

The doctor came into the room and said the lab results showed a very high white blood count due to an infection. He prescribed some antibiotics and gave me some through IV. Once they had finished, I was discharged.

Daddy went by the pharmacy before taking me home to get my medicine. Then he took me home. He stayed with me and Lacy for a while. Dean didn't come straight home from work. That upset Daddy. We put Lacy to bed as he was leaving.

I was walking him to the door, and when I opened it, we saw Dean pull up. He stepped out of the truck, and you could tell that he had been drinking. That made Daddy even more mad. He took his hat off and threw it on the exterior stairs as he ran down them and toward Dean. He swung at Dean but missed. Then Dean swung back. Daddy backed up to avoid the punch and tripped over a bush.

I was crying and yelling for them to stop. Then Daddy looked up at me and said, "You can stay here with him or come home with me."

I immediately asked him, "Are you telling me that I have to choose between my dad or my husband?"

He answered, "Yes, that is how it has to be."

That hurt my heart, but I yelled back, "Well, I guess I don't have a dad anymore if you're making me choose."

I threw his hat at him. Dean came inside, and I slammed the door. Daddy peeled out mad in his truck as he drove away.

I was so mad that I didn't even talk to Dean and just went to bed. Dean tried to apologize, but I didn't want to hear it. I just told him to sober up and we'd talk in the morning.

The next morning we were served with an eviction notice from the noise disturbance between the two of them. What were we going to do now? I had just lost two babies, had a severe infection, and now an eviction.

Dean went to call his mom and see if we could move in with her. She said that was fine if it was temporary.

We put our furniture in storage and moved into a two-bedroom apartment with her and Aaron. They had a pool, so at least we got to relax around there, and Dean taught Lacy how to swim.

He was a good dad when he was present. He liked to drink and didn't come straight home many nights. When he didn't, I'd worry if he'd gone to jail or been in an accident.

Since we were living with his mom, I tried doing most of the cooking and cleaning. However, I couldn't wait to get back into a place of our own.

It was quite embarrassing when Dean would stay out late and sleep all day. If he wasn't sleeping, he was lying on the couch having Lacy get him things from the kitchen, even a gallon of milk, which likely weighed half as much as she did, being she was only two years old at the time.

CHAPTER THIRTY

Finally, we were moving out and getting a place of our own. We didn't have a vehicle. It got repossessed. I got a job at the local grocery store that I could walk to. If it was raining, the owner would pick me up.

Daddy and I still weren't talking. If he wanted to see Lacy, he'd send Anna in to get her. It was rough, and it made me cry every time. I was hoping he'd just give in and realize I wanted to keep my family together.

I was feeling queasy again and took another pregnancy test. Wouldn't you know, it was positive. I made an appointment to see a doctor. Before the date to see the doctor came, I started spotting. A few days later it became a heavy flow. I had a friend take me to the ER, and we found out that I was miscarrying.

I met my neighbor, Marie. She had a daughter a little older than Lacy. Her name was Nicole. Marie was the manager of the town movie rental store. We didn't have cable, so she'd bring us movies to watch, or Lacy and I would go to her house to watch them.

Dean was coming home later and later, drunker and drunker. This was causing a lot of fights between us. He was also becoming abusive. Marie would notice bruises, but I would just make up stories and hoped she would believe them.

I hated leaving Lacy with him during the day, but I had to work, and it was the only way. I was really getting tired of walking every day. I would get picked up some days, it was a small town, and everyone knew everyone.

Eventually we moved into a nice two-bedroom trailer on a corner lot. I wouldn't have to walk as far either. I also felt much safer. There was a nice family restaurant across the street, and the owner told me if I would put in my notice at the store that he would hire me.

I put in my two weeks' notice, and they just let me go. I went over to tell the restaurant owner, and he said he didn't need me after all. Now I was without a job at all. I hadn't spoken with my father in six months, informing him that things were worse for us than before was a hard thing to say. I think he felt sympathy for me, and slowly we began to communicate with each other again. He would come inside when he was there to pick up Lacy for her stay over, and even stayed a few times for dinner.

One night as I was cooking, Leena was over, and I got extremely dizzy. She told me I was pregnant. I didn't think that was it. This was a different feeling.

I took a test the next morning, and it was indeed positive. I just hoped I could carry this one to term.

That day Leena came over to take Dean to his probation appointment. He had missed a few visits, and we were kind of nervous about what the outcome would be.

Dean wasn't with her when she came back. She said they had put him in jail. He wouldn't go to court for a couple of weeks. I was five months pregnant, now had no job, and Dean was in jail.

CHAPTER THIRTY-ONE

The doctor said the sonogram showed a healthy baby boy. I had a garage sale and was getting rid of a lot of baby girl things when for the first time the baby started kicking like crazy!

Leena said, "That's because you are getting rid of her stuff."

I didn't want to believe it was a girl. We really wanted a boy.

April 11, 1994, Dean's court date finally came. It was exactly a year since I lost the twins. Several people testified on his behalf. They all told the judge that they would be sure to get him to his probation appointments, including my dad, his dad, and his boss.

The judge sentenced him to ten years and revoked his probation. I started screaming, "Please, no, I'm pregnant. Don't do this! Give him another chance!"

She had the bailiff remove me from the courtroom. I sat in the hall and cried and cried. Daddy came out with me and tried to calm me down.

He asked me if I wanted to move in with them. I knew he wouldn't allow me to take phone calls from Dean, and he was running in a city election. His place in the election was for city councilman at large. I knew he would be too busy to take me to visit Dean, so I declined.

I was going to move in with Dean's dad and Autumn. It was in the same town we lived in, and Lacy could go to preschool for half a day.

Everyone came together to help me get everything packed up and take most of it to storage. We just took what we needed to Dean's dads.

When it got closer to my due date, I would move in with Mamaw. She lived close to the jail too.

I was in a deep depression with me being pregnant and Dean being in jail. This pregnancy seemed to be going okay at least.

I knew it had been a while since I had been to church. I started reading the Bible again and reading a children's Bible to Lacy. We made sure to say our prayers every night, and she always prayed for God to let her daddy come home. She was a daddy's girl. I felt closer to the Lord again and hoped to stay this way.

Two weeks after the court date, my daddy was taking me to an appointment. He won't be able to wait and bring me home because he needed to take Mama to an appointment. He had asked Dean's dad to pick me up. He walked me inside and gave me a big, tight hug as he told me that he loved me. I sat down and waited to be called back.

After I was done with the appointment, I looked out the window, and Dean Sr. was already waiting for me. Now we would go pick up Lacy and go back to his house and wait for Dean to call me.

Hearing from Dean every day was the only thing that kept me going. I hated being away from him, especially during the pregnancy.

I was tired, so Lacy and I went to bed early. I was awakened by the telephone ringing. I just ignored it and tried to go back to sleep. That didn't work. It just kept ringing. I got up and answered it.

It was Kelly, one of Autumn's friends. She asked to speak to her.

I said, "Kelly, it's four-thirty in the morning. She's asleep." She then asked me if my aunt Vickie had been here yet. "Why would she be coming at this hour?" I asked her. She told me it was because my dad had been in an accident.

About that time there was a knock at the door, so I hung up the phone to answer it. It was Aunt Vickie, and I also saw a figure of a man at the end of the driveway smoking a cigarette.

I asked Aunt Vickie, "What's happened to my daddy? And who is that man?"

She told me that it was Richard, Daddy's friend, and asked me how I knew there was something wrong with him. I told her that Kelly had called.

She told me to wait until we got to the hospital and I would be told everything. I had to wake Autumn up and have her get into bed with Lacy. I also had to put on some clothes.

It was a long, quiet drive to the hospital, and I had a bad feeling in the pit of my stomach. Once we arrived at the hospital, I saw a hearse backed up to the doors of the emergency room. I knew. I just knew my daddy was gone.

I went inside and saw several of our preacher friends and their wives as well as a lot of family members standing in the hallway. I then saw J.R.. I hadn't seen him in years, so that confirmed my conclusion. My daddy had died.

I ran over to J.R. and grabbed him, saying, "Please tell me he's not gone! God already took our mom. He can't have our Daddy too!" After saying that, I heard many break down in tears.

I was so angry and blamed God for taking my daddy. He would never meet this baby. Why? Why did God do this? I felt he was punishing me for something.

"Where's Mama?" I asked. Someone said that she had to be sedated. "What happened to him?" I demanded.

J.R.'s wife, Cindy, was also pregnant and due around the same time. We were both six and a half months along.

My nerves were shot. I asked J.R. for a cigarette and to come outside to tell me what happened. I learned that Daddy couldn't sleep, so he went out to the garage to work on Mama's car. She had said it was making a noise.

Mama had awakened to the sound of a car peeling out from in front of the house. She got out of bed and looked for Daddy. She saw the light in the front yard coming from the opened garage, so she went to the garage.

The car had fallen off the jack and landed on my daddy's chest. Mama found him under the car and ran across the street to get help from the neighbor. They called 911, but it was too late. He was already gone.

Chapter Thirty-Two

I felt a sudden pain shoot through my belly. A few minutes later another one. I was in premature labor. Was I going to lose this baby too? Uncle Jean and his second wife, Aunt Faye, took me inside to be seen.

The nurse hooked me up to the monitor, and indeed I was having contractions. The baby's heart rate was also low. I cried hysterically, and the heart rate went even lower.

Suddenly a peace came over me, and the heart rate went up. I felt as if my daddy had told me to "calm down or you're going to lose this baby. You must stay calm for the safety of the baby." I felt that he was telling me he was okay and not to worry and to focus on the health of the baby.

The doctor came back in to tell me this hospital did not treat premature births and he was going to transfer me to another hospital that would. Aunt Faye asked if she and Uncle Jean could drive me there, and the doctor said that they could.

Uncle Jean pulled the car up, and Aunt Faye helped me get in, and we were off to the hospital. From here, it's just a blur. The doctor kept me sedated and was able to stop my labor.

I remember Dean's mom coming and telling me that she and Dean Sr. went to visit Dean and let him know about my dad. I also remember my cousin Joe coming to see me because I thought he was Daddy. He looked so much like him. I know Aunt Faye never left my side.

The day I was getting discharged was the day of the funeral. The doctor wasn't going to let me go to the funeral, but I told him there was no way that I was missing my daddy's funeral. He gave me a pill and told me to take it before the funeral to keep me calm.

Dean's dad took me to Mama and Daddy's house. It was very weird being here without Daddy. We were waiting for the limo to drive us to the church.

Once the limo got there, Mama, Anna, J.R., Cindy, and I all climbed inside. It was a very quiet and long ride. There were a lot of vehicles that followed us to the church.

When I walked into the church, Dean was the first person I saw. I went to him, and he hugged me tightly. He was dressed in a nice suit but was escorted by sheriff deputies. They had let him out for the funeral because my dad was a sheriff officer.

There were so many people there that not everyone fit inside the church. The officers were kind enough not to cuff Dean, allowed him to sit with me during the service, and he got to ride in the limo to the graveside.

On the way to the cemetery, we saw people on the side of the road taking their hats off. The procession was at least two miles long. He was very well known. There were firefighters and sheriff officers there as he was both.

It was so sad when the officers came up to Dean and told him it was time to go. I wasn't ready to say goodbye to him. I had just buried my daddy. The officers apologized but said he had to go. Dean and I both broke down. It wasn't fair.

We took the limo back to Mama and Daddy's and ate lunch with some friends and family. I went to Daddy's closet and sat on the floor with the door closed. Not long after, Anna joined me. We each took one of his shirts and wrapped it around us. I was twenty, and she was only sixteen.

I heard someone looking for me, so I got up out of the closet. It was Autumn. She and her dad were going home and wanted to know if I was too. I was ready to get out of this house. I gave Anna a hug and told her to call anytime.

When we got home, I changed my clothes and went straight to bed. It was a very exhausting day. Leena was keeping Lacy for a few more days.

Dean and I talked on the phone every night. It was cheaper for him to call Mamaw's house than his dad's. I was close to the hospital and was due in nine and a half weeks. Lacy loved staying there too.

Daddy's death was so close to the election. They had not enough time to remove his name from the ballot. He was such an upstanding man in the county. He was a firefighter for twenty-seven years, a peace officer for twelve years, a certified emergency medical technician, a sheriff's officer for ten years (six years of that as an assistant director), and a city police officer for two years. With all this knowledge and popularity, he would have been an asset for the role of city councilman at large.

He was the first dead man on a ballot to win an election in the county. Mama would have the chance to accept the role, or it would be passed on to someone else. When she was interviewed, she turned down the position. They would elect someone else, but he made history and would always be remembered in the county.

We had Mama's car taken to an auto repair. While it was on the lift, we videoed the mechanic pointing out where the jack had been kicked out from under the car. Also, he told us that he couldn't see where any repairs were recently made, and nothing was wrong with the car. The next week the mechanic was shot and killed.

While staying at Mamaw's, we were getting threatening phone calls and learned Daddy was too. In fact, he called the man in the election for mayor the night of his death and told him he had just received a threatening call, describing what he was wearing and to watch over his shoulder.

Several of us were digging, trying to find out what happened. There were a few of us staying at Mamaw's when we got a call that said that we needed to stop poking around or someone would get hurt. When we went to the police, they tapped the phone, and the calls stopped. Was the police department corrupt? Did someone on the force know something.

Chapter Thirty-Three

It was August 18, 1994, and I had a doctor appointment. He said I could go into the hospital to be induced tomorrow. I went to Mamaw's and started packing a bag. Dean called, and I got to tell him the news. I was excited, so I called Beth to see if she would take me to the hospital. Really, I could walk. It would be good exercise.

I found out J.R.'s wife, Cindy, had a baby boy, yet she was expecting a girl. Autumn joked that I would have a girl.

Anna and Autumn were both sixteen, the same age I was when I got pregnant with Lacy. I wanted both to go into the delivery room with me. I thought maybe that might discourage them from having kids at their age after witnessing a childbirth.

It seemed this delivery was going a lot faster. Before I knew it, I was ready to start pushing. The nurse told me to give it one more big push on the next contraction. I did, and the baby was born. I heard a cry. Then the nurse said, "It's a girl!" I just fell back onto the bed. I was expecting a boy. I received everything for a boy at the shower. Even Aunt Faye had made Cindy a baby book for a girl and me one for a boy. We would switch those, I suppose.

What a strange thing for Autumn to foretell, my sister-in-law expecting a girl and having a boy, myself having a girl while expecting a boy. With the simple exchange of outfits to right the situation, I laughingly had the feeling that Daddy was having some fun with this.

I called the jail, and they were going to let Dean call me. When he called, I cried, "It's a girl, you won't divorce me right?"

He laughed. "Of course not. It's our daughter."

What were we going to name her? He told me he always liked the name Lana. It sounded like Anna, and since they were in the delivery room, it would be nice to name her after both.

"How about Lana Faith?"

That was Autumn's middle name. I always really liked it. He said that he loved it. Lana Faith weighed eight pounds and one ounce. The exact weight as Lacy. When the nurse cleaned her up and put her on my belly, it was like seeing and holding Lacy at her birth.

Everyone came in, and I introduced them to Lana Faith. The nurse took a picture of us all. We could barely fit in the photo.

Leena brought Lacy up the next morning to meet her little sister. She was instantly in love with her. The first thing she asked though, was, "I thought she was going to be a boy." I told her that she tricked us all.

Later that day, Cindy and I walked the hall together. She had a C-section, so she was a little slower than I was. We just traded outfits and car seats. When we were released, we were going to trade everything else. Including the baby books Aunt Faye had made us.

Two days later, we both got to go home with the babies. Thankfully they were both healthy, especially after the stress of Daddy's death. He would have been overjoyed with two grandbabies born thirty-six hours apart in the same hospital.

Dean did not want to see Lana for the first time through glass and be unable to hold her. I understood that. He had been put on a work release program. After he'd done it awhile, he thought we could eat lunch with him, and he could hold Lana then and visit Lacy too.

Grandmother called to ask me to guess who she had seen today. It was Dean. She saw these guys working so hard in the hot sun and took them some iced tea. One of the guys was Dean.

The girls and I would go over there for lunch the next day. She told the foreman he was married to her granddaughter and he had never got to hold his newborn daughter. He told her that Dean could go over there for lunch.

I was so happy when he knocked on the door. We hadn't been able to touch since Daddy's funeral. I gave him a big kiss then took him to meet his daughter.

He and I both cried as he held her for the first time. She was almost a month old. He didn't get to hold her long as he still had to see Lacy and eat lunch too. He only got thirty minutes with us. I didn't want him to go back. Lacy and I both cried when he had to go back.

We had planned to go back the next day, but Grandmother's nosey neighbor called and told the jail. They took him off that job site. I really wanted to go give her a piece of my mind, but Grandmother told me to leave well enough alone. They might not let him do work release again if I didn't.

I moved back in with his dad, so Lacy could go to preschool. Lana was keeping me up at night. She was colicky and cried all the time. I was suffering from postpartum depression. I just couldn't take it anymore.

I went to my room and cried uncontrollably. Autumn came in to check on me. I told her I couldn't do it alone anymore and I wanted to die. I was not a good mother, and the girls deserved better. She told me to go to a friend's house or take a drive, to get away by myself, and she would watch the girls. Also, that she would help me out more so that I didn't feel so alone.

Finally, after three weeks, he felt comfortable with his new foreman to ask if we could come for lunch. He agreed to let us.

It was the first time Dean got to feed Lana. Lacy was ecstatic to see her dad and get to give him hugs and kisses. I was happy to kiss him too.

After a visit on Friday, October 28, 1994, Dean called me to tell me that sheriff officers had come to the work site looking for him while he was with me. We would have to wait until Monday to see what they wanted.

Dean called me Monday morning to come pick him up. He was getting out. I wouldn't be a single parent anymore. Leena agreed to watch the girls until we got back so we could surprise Lacy.

Dean drove us to Leena's. He said that he felt so free. Lacy was so happy to see her daddy. To know that he would be home with us again was the best feeling.

CHAPTER THIRTY-FOUR

It's February 1995. Lacy is four, and we moved out so we would have our own place. Anna moved in with us, and Dean got a job as a store manager for a burger and gas company. He was making pretty good money; we had a nice place. Everything seemed to be finally going well.

Dean started going out again after work, not coming home until the wee hours of the morning drunk. We fought a lot.

The threatening phone calls had started coming again, which is strange because we just moved, and I got a new phone number. I knew they've started up because we had gotten a court order to have Daddy's body exhumed for an autopsy. I didn't understand why one wasn't done after his death.

I had started smoking cigarettes again due to all the stress I had been dealing with for months and Dean staying out all night all the time. This was something that I never thought I would do again after becoming a mom, but Dean and I were fighting quite a bit.

I felt like praying and asking for God's help didn't work anymore. Like he'd been punishing me my whole life. I guess I should thank him for the hard times as well as the good. For it was through those times he gave me strength to make it through the times yet to come.

I've started feeling queasy again. I took a pregnancy test, and it's positive. *Again? We've tried to be careful. How can this be?* I stopped smoking cold turkey. I wouldn't do it knowing I was pregnant.

I got in to see the doctor as soon as possible. He went ahead and did a sonogram since his measurements were questionable. The sonogram showed I was a little over four months along. Oh no! Had I harmed the baby by smoking? The doctor says it looks to be a very healthy boy.

Well, I was glad it's healthy, but I was not falling for believing it's a boy again. We'd see when it's born. It was going to be a short pregnancy anyways.

Daddy's autopsy came back as inconclusive. The casket was not sealed properly and waterlogged. The body was more decomposed than it normally should be. Was it not sealed properly intentionally? Did someone cover their tracks that well?

I was scared for our lives. The threats got worse. I called the police. Once again, the calls quit when a tap was placed on the phone. It was as if someone knew our every move and was one step ahead of us.

Anna came home from school one day and was screaming for me as she got out of her car. I went out to see what was wrong, and she was crying out, "She married him! She married him! Mama married him!" She was referring to Daddy's friend, Richard.

I told her to go inside with the girls. I was going over to his house to confront them. When I got there, they both came to the door with a closed screen. I started yelling at Mama, asking, "How could you marry him?" I accused them of murdering Daddy, calling them both murderers and inappropriate names.

Richard came out, pushing me off the porch while tightly grabbing my arm and directing me to my car as I asked him, "You were supposed to be my daddy's best friend. How could you do this?"

He asked, "Did you want your mom to be alone for the rest of her life?"

I snapped back hastefully, "Of course not, but not with you."

He told me to leave his property before he called the police. I told him to go ahead and I'd tell them how they murdered my dad. I felt he was a little rough with me being pregnant. I just left. It wasn't worth it.

I really think Richard had something to do with Daddy's death. There were other possibilities though. Daddy was running in that election and had uncovered crooked things the mayor of twenty years was doing. All I knew was that my dad's death was no accident and they had closed the case. It was as if no one cared to find out the truth.

The tap was removed, and the calls were coming in again. This time I had a recorder by the phone and recorded a couple. The recordings didn't pick up the sound very well though.

CHAPTER THIRTY-FIVE

I was twenty-four weeks along and woke up to my water leaking. I had Anna stay with the girls while Dean took me to the hospital.

Once we got there and saw the doctor, he confirmed it was amniotic fluid leaking. He wanted to send me to a specialty hospital by ambulance. I was also having contractions.

Dean followed the ambulance to the hospital, which was two hours away. The doctor came in right away when we arrived. He was able to stop the contractions and give me steroid shots to help build up the baby's lungs in case I delivered early.

He suggested I get them every two weeks until the baby's birth. I was released the next day. They said I might continue to have minimal leakage through the rest of the pregnancy and to take it as easy as possible.

When we got home, both girls were happy to see us. Lacy asked me, "Where's my baby brother?"

I told her he wouldn't be here for a couple of months.

Our place had only two bedrooms. There was Lacy's toddler bed, Lana's crib, and Anna's twin bed in the second bedroom. Then mine and Dean's bedroom had our king waterbed in it, but we had a huge closet and were planning to put a crib in it too.

We were going to make it work. I loved living there. It was off the road in the country in a little triplex and convenient to the interstate. Dean's mom lived close by as well as Leena. Autumn and her boyfriend stopped by frequently too. I loved having Anna there. She was a Junior in high school.

It was time for my third steroid shot. Luckily, my local doctor was able to give them to me, so I didn't have to go out of town for them. Dean went with me. They usually did a sonogram to make sure I wasn't losing too much amniotic fluid and the baby was growing properly.

Everything looked good for twenty-eight weeks along, the doctor said. I was still leaking, but it was very minimal, and the baby was looking very healthy and growing quickly. He still wanted me to take it as easy as possible.

The next afternoon I began to have contractions. Dean took me to the hospital. It was just Braxton-Hicks, thank goodness. I did not want the baby to be born yet. It was too soon.

The baby wasn't due until September 21, which was Dean's mom's birthday. I'd like to at least make it to the second week of September.

August 12, I went in for my steroid shot and sonogram. The doctor came in and suggested we go ahead and induce. What? Lana wasn't even a year old.

"By the looks of the sonogram, the baby weighs about eleven pounds," said the doctor. "If you go to term, it could be over thirteen pounds."

He also told us the sonogram could be off by three pounds either way. He wanted to meet me at the hospital the next afternoon at five o'clock. The baby would be six weeks early.

The next afternoon, the nurses got me all hooked up to the machines. I was already having contractions on my own. They wanted to see how I could progress without being induced. The nurse came in about nine o'clock and gave me oxytocin because the contractions just stopped and I wasn't getting anywhere. Another hour went by, and I hadn't progressed, so the doctor broke my water. Not long after that, contractions picked up. Around one o'clock the anesthesiologist gave me an epidural.

The next thing I remember it was daylight, and the nurse was checking me and said I was ready now.

"Really?" I asked.

I yelled at Dean to wake up. We were ready to have a baby. This was the first time he had been in the delivery room with me. He held my hand, and the doctor entered, telling me to push.

A few more pushes and the baby was born. The doctor said, "Congratulations! It's a boy!" I remember saying, "Thank you, God." Then Dean said, "I finally got my boy."

The nurse cleaned him up and handed him to Dean, saying, "You have a healthy boy weighing eight pounds eight ounces, and twenty-two inches long." Dean just took him from her, saying nothing, just smiling.

"What do we name him?" I asked.

Dean answered, "I have always loved David."

I liked it too, but what about his middle name? "How about David James?" I asked him.

"Perfect." He agreed.

Dean called his mom and told her the news. She called Anna to get the girls ready to meet their brother. Lacy loved him immediately. Lana, not so much. She smacked him in the face. Hopefully, that would not be a regular thing. She would be a year old in five days. We had our twins after all, just Irish twins instead.

Anna and Autumn came to meet their nephew. They teased Dean, saying he waited to be in the delivery room until he finally had a boy. He laughed and kind of agreed with them.

The nurse came to get me for surgery. Now that we finally had our boy, I was getting my tubes tied. We weren't going to chance it again. The doctor said surgery would be about forty-five minutes. The anesthesiologist told me to count backward from ten. I remember 6 being the last number. Dean said that I didn't even wake up when they came in to take my vitals. I was very exhausted.

After two days, we finally got to go home. I was glad that I got that extra sleep. David was worse than Lana. He cried all the time. Sometimes he woke up every hour. It was very exhausting.

Lana was finally sleeping all night. I think God had a hand in that, knowing two babies waking up throughout the night would be too much.

For Lana's birthday party, I had Anna go pick up some gifts for me. Beth ordered a cake. Dean fixed up a wall of balloons for a lucky dart game, plus pin the tail on the donkey too. I was not getting around well at all. The tubal ligation surgery was rough. Having Anna around was a big help. We put her in her high chair, on top of newspapers to catch the mess, then sat the cake down with a candle lit on it. We quickly sang "Happy Birthday" as she wanted that cake. Dean took the cake and cut a fourth of it off for Lana to dig into. It was the funniest thing. She was shaking, but once she got a taste of that cake, it was all she wanted. So focused on eating it up.

Once she had enough, Dean took her to the bathroom and gave her a bath. She had cake all over her. Since I had the surgery, I couldn't pick her up, and neither of us could stand that. Dean put her on the bed so that I could dress her.

A couple from out of town, Robert and Shawna, came to visit us. Dean said it would be good for me to get out of the house and he would watch all the kids, so she and I went to Walmart and picked up a few things. When we came back, I saw many vehicles parked at my house. Dean had arranged a surprise baby shower for me. He even had Grandmother there. Mamaw and Aunt Elsa were there too. I was quite elated.

I received a lot of baby boy stuff, which was good since I had practically none. David's outfits were very cute. Dean had arranged for decorations, food, and cake. Of course he had help, but I was really surprised that he'd pulled it off. He'd never done anything like this before.

It was nice to have all the grandparents at our house at the same time. Never had any of them been to our house before.

CHAPTER THIRTY-SIX

It was the first part of September, and I was still recovering from my surgery when I heard Dean scream for me at the back door. It went down into a dark storage room, which was where we kept our trash until trash day.

He hollered for me to grab a kitchen towel and wrap it tightly around his calf and hold it tightly while he tried to make it up into the kitchen.

Once we got him into the kitchen light, he saw how bad it was. He picked up a trash bag against his leg. Something sharp had cut him from ankle to knee badly. I grabbed a bigger towel, held it on his leg, and helped him get into the car. Then I went inside and told Anna that I was taking him to the ER.

I wasn't even supposed to be driving for two more weeks, but he had to be seen. He wouldn't even let me see it but told me it was bad. I believed it was by the amount of blood I could see soaking into the towel.

When we arrived at the hospital, I went in to get some help and a wheelchair. I finally saw it when the doctor came in to stitch him up. It took three layers of stitches, at around one-hundred and eighty of them the doctor lost count.

We were at the hospital for what seemed like forever. I called Anna and told her what was going on and to call Dean's mom and tell her what happened. After an IV of antibiotics, his leg wrapped in fresh bandage and a tetanus shot, we were finally able to go home.

When we got there, and Dean's mom had come to help us out, she made him a pallet in the living room because getting in and out of our waterbed was going to be too hard for him. She stayed with us for a few days to help since I couldn't pick up Lana and Dean had to stay off the leg. He wasn't going to be able to work for six weeks.

Once I had my four-week checkup, I went looking for work. I found a job the first day at a nice bar and grill. It was a place with an expensive menu. I was sure to make good tips.

I just hated going to work while David was so young. Leena helped with the kids while I worked until Dean was better. Sometimes I had to work split shifts, so I would go to Mamaw's during my break since it was just up the road.

I had worked here for a little over a year when I got a call from Anna one day. She told me I might want to come home. I asked her if the kids were okay. She assured me what was going on had nothing to do with Dean or the kids.

I was so worried all the way home. I was surprised I arrived safely because I didn't even remember the drive. When I got in the house, Anna told me to sit down.

"Just please tell me what is going on," I told her.

She then told me that my grandmother had passed away. She had told me when I was pregnant with David that she would live long enough to meet all my kids. She was eighty-two years old and had done what she said she would do. David had just turned one. I had been worried that she wouldn't make it that long since Granddaddy had passed away a little over a year ago. He was eighty-seven. She had kept her word. Just as she always did.

One day on my way to work, a man ran a stop sign and hit my car. I was only two blocks from work. A coworker saw me at the accident and stopped to check on me. My shoulder was slammed into the window, and my hand was numb. She went to tell the boss and gave me a ride to the ER.

The doctor came in and ordered x-rays. My shoulder was dislocated and must have been pinching a nerve. He popped my shoulder into place and gave me a sling and a couple of prescriptions. Looks like I was out of work again for a while.

My coworker took me home. I barely remember the ride because they had given me pain meds at the hospital.

She helped me inside, gave Dean an update, and headed back to work.

Later that day we got a call from the body shop that the car was totaled. I really hated that since I'd just bought it before Lana was born.

After a few months of seeing a specialist and receiving injections in my shoulder, I was allowed to return to work. I also received a settlement from the accident.

A few days later, I went to work, and there was a note on the door that read, "Our doors have permanently closed. Our apologies for any inconveniences."

What? No way! I loved this job and made great money here. The door was unlocked, so I went inside. The manager was seated at the bar. She asked me to sit down. After I sat down, she informed me that corporate had decided to close our doors. She handed me my paycheck along with a $500 severance pay.

I went out to the car and prayed for God to put another opportunity in my life, thanking him for providing for us even in difficult times. After that, I drove home to tell the family.

Chapter Thirty-Seven

The landlords had decided to sell the place and gave us thirty days to move out, and I still hadn't found a job. What were we going to do? I asked God to please help us keep a roof over the family's heads. I had complete faith that he would provide for us as he had always done in the past. He had shown his presence even in difficult times.

While I was out job hunting one day, I ran into a friend that I had met when I was in inpatient therapy as a teen named Penny. I told her we were going to have to move. Just so happened her second house was vacant and for sale. It was a two-story old Victorian style home and would be a great deal for us.

The only bad thing was it would be out of our county lines and Dean was still on parole. He said we would look at it anyways. When we pulled up to the house, we were in awe at its size. It was very nice with four bedrooms, two bath.

We brought Anna with us to look at the house as well as the kids. When we got back outside, Lana started screaming loudly. We looked down, and her legs were covered in fleas. We checked our legs, and they were also covered. Even our jeans were black instead of blue from all the fleas. Other than that, we loved the house.

I called Penny to let her know, and she said that she would take care of them for us. We had to decide quickly though, or she was going to a realtor. Now to figure out what to do about Dean's parole. If we were to ask for a transfer to a different county, it could take months.

The next day I went to see Mamaw and Elsa. I told them about the house, which was literally only blocks away from them over the county line. I asked them if we could give their address as our residence and if parole came by that all they had to do was call and we'd get here. They both agreed to it and seemed happy for us about the house.

I called Penny and told her that we would take it. We began to move that weekend. I wondered if we would have enough furniture to fill it because it was so big. The kids loved having so much room to run around in.

I finally found a job a few blocks away, bartending at a bar and grill. It was good money too. I thanked the Lord. Once again, he had provided a way for us like he always did.

Dean's aunt Gina and her two kids, Jimmy and Noel, had gotten evicted from their home. She worked a short distance from the house and one day asked if they could move in with us until she was able to get back on her feet. Of course we agreed. It would also mean more help around the house and kids for us.

Dean's friend, Bill, had a pool table and nowhere to keep it, so Dean let him keep it at our house. We had room for it, but that meant Dean would always be having parties and people over all hours of the night.

We fought about this all the time. The kids were upstairs asleep thankfully through most of the fights. Dean became abusive. One afternoon we had plans to go out. Then his friend Allen came over, and they decided that they were going out. I was so mad and hurt that I called work and asked if they could use some help. I was in the bathroom getting ready, and he came in to see what I was doing. He closed the door behind him. I told him if he was going out, I was going to work. He pushed me into the toilet and busted my head.

It wasn't bad, so I got the bleeding to stop and left for work. Once I made it there, I just sat in the car and cried. I was blaming God! Couldn't he just bring Wes back into my life. I tried to be a good wife. Why was Dean so mean to me? Why didn't he really love me? Was I not a good wife?

Dean didn't come home at all one night. I got on the phone and started calling hospitals. There were none that had him, so I called the jail. He was arrested on a warrant for violating parole.

My aunt Elsa had told the parole officer that he did not live there. I was so mad, after all she told me she would say that he did. I went to Mamaw's house and angrily confronted Aunt Elsa. I told her that she could have told me she didn't want to help us, and I could have made other arrangements. Now he was back in jail, and I had three kids who miss their daddy. She told me she was not apologizing and that I never should have asked her to cover for him. She told me that she had nothing else to say to me and to leave.

I continued working evenings, and Gina worked days. Anna kept David and Lana during the day so I could get some rest. Lacy was in school now. Gina cooked dinner for everyone when she got home. We made it work with the three of us, and Jimmy helped a lot too.

A few weeks after Dean's arrest, he was released. The only thing was we had to move back to the county. Sadly, we would have to leave the house that we all loved. Gina had to find a place for her, Noel, and Jimmy to live, and Anna had to find a place as well.

We were going to move back in with Dean's dad. I had to quit my job because I would be unable to get back and forth. The only good thing about moving back into Dean's dad's was that I got to be close to Autumn again.

CHAPTER THIRTY-EIGHT

When we moved back in with Dean's dad, I looked for work nearby. Dean went back to work at the burger place. Luckily, I was able to find a job at the local grocery store. Autumn watched the kids while we worked. Working at the grocery store wasn't so bad. I worked from seven o'clock in the morning until three-thirty in the afternoon. Dean usually had to be at work at four o'clock in the afternoon, so we really didn't see each other.

I'd gotten a call from a mutual friend of mine and Dean's. She said that Dean had been coming to her house with a young girl. Autumn watched the kids and let me use her car to go confront him at his job. Once I got there, I asked him to come outside. When he came out, I asked, "Are you having an affair? I want the truth." Of course he denied it. I told him that I would be gone when he came home and then left.

I sat in the car and cried before praying for God to once again give me a clue of what to do. Then I thought of Monica, a girl from work. She had two children and a big house. Maybe we could stay with her for a while. We'd gotten to know each other well. I went inside and called her. I told her what was going on and asked if we could stay with them for a while. Her oldest was in school with Lacy, and she worked the same hours I did.

I asked Leena if she could watch Lana and David for me when I worked. She just lived just minutes from Monica, so that worked out. Her husband made sure Lacy and their son got on the school bus.

It wasn't uncomfortable at their house, but I was always thinking of Dean and that girl, especially since he hadn't even looked for us. One night while Bryan, Monica's husband, was home, we went to Dean's job around the time for him to get off to spy on him. A young girl got in the car with him. We followed them. They went to a house not far from there, and both went inside.

Monica and I waited across the street to see if or when he came back out. He came out two hours later alone. We followed him and saw that he went home. We went back to Monica's and went to bed.

The next day we were both off. I helped Monica clean the house and fix the kids some lunch. I went to my bedroom while the kids took a nap and prayed, "Dear God, forgive me where I have sinned. Please help me to save my family. Show Dean the path to take to be the husband and father he is meant to be. I ask this in your name, Amen."

After Lacy and Cole, Monica's son, came home from school, I helped them with homework while she fixed dinner. Leena knew where I was staying, and I had given her Monica's phone number. She called and told me that Dean was looking for me. He wanted to talk. I told her to tell him to come to my work tomorrow when I got off.

Monica and I went back up to Dean's job to see if he left with the girl again. I had to know before I talked to him. When Dean came out, he was alone. He got in the car and drove toward his dad's. We followed him. He went straight home.

We went back to Monica's and tried to get some sleep. We both had to work tomorrow. I could not sleep. I was wondering how my conversation would go with Dean the next day. Monica and I were awake and getting everyone ready for work and school. We dropped Lana and David off at Leena's, and I let her know that I would be late picking them up. She was fine with that and offered to pick up Lacy from school as well.

I was dreaded work that day. I knew my mind would be elsewhere. Monica told me to just think positive and focus on stocking as it was delivery day. The truck was a big load that day, so it kept me occupied. While I was working on my aisle, a cashier asked if I could help a customer find an item. I went to the aisle to meet the customer. It was Jolie. My heart literally jumped out of my chest. We had not spoken since the day I found out she married Richard. I was the supervisor on duty, so I had no choice but to help her. When she told me what she was looking for, it happened to be something we did not carry. What a relief, I got to walk away from that one.

Before I realized, it was the end of my shift. I clocked out and looked for Dean. He was sitting in the car. I went to the passenger side and got in. He thanked me for talking to him and told me he missed us. He also said we could move so the girl wouldn't know where we lived, and he would even transfer stores. It all sounded good to me. I missed us too. I told him to start looking for a place and reach out to Leena. Then I would come back.

Even though I wanted to go right then, something pulled me back. I needed a safe place, he didn't know where Monica lived, and I wanted to keep it that way.

Monica and I went to pick up Lana and David over at Leena's. We made sure Dean wasn't following us too. After we ate, got the kids bathed and put to bed, we asked Bryan to watch the kids one more time. Monica didn't think it hurt to make sure Dean wasn't lying to me. He got in the car alone and went straight home, which made me feel he really wanted us to work out. I would wait for him to contact Leena again.

The next morning Leena called and said Dean had called her again. Monica and I were off, so once we had gotten the kids on the bus, I packed up our stuff, and she took us to Leena's house.

I thanked her, and she said we were welcome anytime. I went inside and called Dean. I told him that we were at Leena's. He was off from work today too. He said he found us a house a block from his dad's. Leena watched Lana and David, so we could go look at it.

It was a nice mobile home and looked brand-new. It was also a great deal along with being close to Dean Sr.'s. We paid the deposit, and the landlord said we could pay the prorated rent when we moved in.

We went to pick up the kids. They were so happy to see their daddy. We told them we were moving into our own house soon and we were going to take them to see it. They were so excited to hear the good news.

We took them to see the house and showed them their rooms. They loved it and wanted to know when we were moving in. We told them that we could move in this weekend.

The prorated rent was paid and utilities turned on. It was moving day for us. It was going to be a long day. All our stuff was in storage, and we had to borrow a truck. After the last load was unloaded, Dean went to get a pizza from the grocery store deli while I gave the kids a bath and fixed up their rooms a little.

Dean got back, and I stopped long enough to eat. He knew me, and since I was off tomorrow, I wouldn't stop until we were unpacked. He helped me. Usually unpacking was not his thing. Was this a sign of good things to come?

CHAPTER THIRTY-NINE

December 1999, Lacy was almost nine, Lana was five, and David was four. Lacy was having a Christmas play at school. Lana was not feeling well, so Dean was going to stay home with her and David. I rode to the play with Beth and Autumn. We finished earlier than planned. When we were driving up to my house, we saw a car parked across the street. As we got closer, I noticed that it was that young girl's car.

I called the house from the cell phone I now had and went and stood by her car. When Dean answered, I told him to send her outside. He asked where I was, and I said I was waiting for her by her car. I could see her in the windows of my house running from the front door to the back door unsure what to do.

Beth waited for her to come out and kept Lacy in the car with her. When she, now I know as Rita, finally came out running to her car, I lunged toward her and was pulled back by one of Dean's friends. Beth came over, put her finger in his face, and told him to let me go, that this was not his business. He let me go, and I screamed at her as she got in her car and locked the door. I went to the passenger side calling her a home wrecker. Another girl was with her and had climbed in the passenger seat. I tried to climb over her to get to Rita, screaming the whole time. Dean's friend grabbed me again, and Rita started to leave. Beth was driving slow in front of her and keeping her from getting too far. I threw rocks at her back window. She drove away, and I could not keep up.

The police showed up because the landlord called them. Dean was arrested because of a traffic ticket warrant. Then another officer ran my information, and I had a warrant too for an unpaid ticket for no insurance, which turned out to be a clerical error on their part. Dean's uncle Graham was at the house and said he would watch Lana and David until one of us could get back.

Thank goodness the officer knew me and put me in the front seat of his car and did not cuff me. I called a friend, Deana, from work to come to pick me up. The officer said if I could prove I had paid it, we would get the money back. Deana felt guilty since she knew Dean and got him out too.

That was an awkward ride home. He just kept saying that nothing was going on between them. I did not respond. I just looked up at the sky asking God, *What do I do now?* I slept on the couch that night.

It was almost Christmas, and I couldn't go through a separation during the holidays. What would that do to the kids? I prayed to God, "Show me the answers. Did I need to leave Dean for good, or would he change? I need your guidance. Why do I keep going down the wrong path? Do I have blinders on? If so, God please take them off so I can see clearly. In Jesus's name, amen."

The next morning, the landlords came over with an eviction notice. We had to be out in thirty days. Here we go again. I was getting tired of this song and dance.

Our car was broken down, and Dean had "found a bicycle," so he said. A nice one too. We got into an argument because of the eviction. He went outside and was going to ride off on that bicycle, so I yelled out the door, "Guess I'll call the cops and tell them that you are on a stolen bike!" Then I ran back inside and locked the door.

He banged on it loudly and tried to yank it open, so I unlocked it and tried to run away. We had never argued in front of the kids like this before. Uncle Graham thankfully took them to their room. Dean came inside, grabbed my hair, pulled me to him, then pushed me down. I sat up, and blood was pouring out of my head.

I went into the bathroom, and it looked as if I didn't have an eye. I put a towel with a lot of pressure on my eye. Dean came to the bathroom door and begged me to let him in. I wouldn't do it. I told him to go away, that he had hurt me badly. He knew it and didn't mean to. He said to let him look at it. I opened the door and removed the towel. I knew it was bad. He borrowed his uncle Graham's car and took me to the ER.

I couldn't tell them what really happened, so I said I tripped carrying groceries inside on the door threshold and landed on my face on the kitchen floor. It took three layers of stitches to sew it up. I was told to keep ice on it and rest. Why did I keep covering for him?

Dean was at my beck and call. He felt so bad, which he should. Uncle Graham had cleaned up the blood so the kids wouldn't be so traumatized. I called in to work and told them I would probably be out a week but would keep them posted.

We were able to stay in the mobile home until the one Dean would buy was delivered and set up. It would be in the mobile home park next door after the New Year. Hopefully 2000 would be a better year.

I went back to work. My boss pulled me to the side and asked if I was being abused. I didn't want people knowing, so of course I made up excuses for Dean as I always did.

It's now February 2000. It was finally moving day. Since things with Dean had been on and off, I did not cosign for our mobile home. It was snowing, which was making the move a little challenging. The new place was just on the other side of a small field, the kids were having a blast and carrying things from house to house in the snow.

As we were moving in, the mobile home company was putting the under pending on. All the utilities had been turned on, and since the homes were so close to another, I was moving and unpacking one room at a time.

After everything was unloaded and unpacked, Dean, the kids, and I had a picnic on the living room floor and watched a movie. The kids fell asleep, and I almost did too. Dean took the kids and put them in their beds. He and I would have to sleep in the living room until our waterbed was filled and heated.

The ground was covered with snow the next morning. The kids spent most of the day playing in it. I had to go to the other house to clean it and return the keys.

That afternoon we used a plastic kiddie swimming pool and pushed the kids down a hill inside it. Oh, what fun, they were loving it. We also used a plastic trash can lid as a sled. Dean pushed me down the hill on it, and I ran over something and really hurt my bottom. I wanted to do it again, so we moved over a little so I wouldn't run over it again, but the lid veered over some, and I ran over it again. This time it really hurt, and I heard something pop. I couldn't even get up, so I just rolled over and lay on the ground.

Dean helped me into the house. I was in so much pain. I just lay on the couch all night almost in tears. Dean fixed the kids' dinner then hot chocolate and a movie.

I could barely get up the next day. Dean thought I might have just bruised my tailbone, so we were going to give it a couple of days.

A couple of days had gone by, and I wasn't any better. One of my friends took me to the ER, and I had broken the tip of my tailbone right off. The doctor gave me a prescription for pain and a donut to sit on.

When I got home, I had Dean help me get into the tub after I had taken a pain pill. I sat on my donut and soaked for a while. It felt nice, and the pain eased up. When I got ready to get out, I had Dean come into the bathroom.

He jerked me up so fast that I passed out. He rolled me in a blanket and took me to Lacy's bed.

I slept for a couple of hours. When I woke up, there were so many people over. I was so embarrassed that I didn't even look to see who was there. I had to walk through the living room wrapped up in a blanket. I called him into the bedroom and had him help me get dressed.

After I got dressed, I went back into the living room. Deana and her husband, Collin, were over as well as Bill and Kevin, a couple of Dean's friends that I really didn't care for. Thankfully, Kevin and Bill left. Deana was more my friend. She would even babysit the kids for me when I was working.

I got my donut and sat on the couch and was visiting with Deana when Dean said that Rita was accusing me of busting out the window of her car. Supposedly this had happened while I was in no condition to have done that.

I thought this meant that he had seen her again.

Deana and Collin stayed for dinner. After we ate, I went to the kids' bedroom and tucked them in, and before we said our prayers, David asked if we could pray for my bottom. He always said the cutest thing and was a very thoughtful little boy.

CHAPTER FORTY

Anna had a new boyfriend named Mitch. She and he stopped by one day and asked if she could stay with us for a while. She also told us that she was pregnant. I was happy for her. Apparently, they had been seeing each other for a while.

She stayed with us for a couple of months, and that gave Deana a break from babysitting the kids. It would keep Anna busy too. Mitch was going to work and save up some money to get them their own place.

Things had been going well for Dean and me lately. I hadn't heard anything from or saw Rita in months. It was now early September 2000. All the kids were in school. David was five and in kindergarten, Lana six and in first grade, and Lacy was nine and in the fourth grade. I was still working at the local grocery store as a supervisor, and Dean was still at the burger place. Anna and Mitch had gotten their own place about an hour away from us.

We had gotten a computer, and sometimes at night I would stay up and play Slingo. I had recently signed up for Classmates.com to reconnect with old classmates as my class reunion would be soon.

One night I could not sleep so I got up to play Slingo and check my emails. I had an email from Classmates.com that someone wanted to connect with me. I opened it and noticed that it was Wes. I figured it would be nice to catch up with him, so I accepted. He was online, so we began chatting as I played Slingo.

Dean came into the living room and asked what I was doing. I told him I was playing Slingo. He came over to the computer and about that time a message from Wes popped up on the screen. He read it and saw who I was chatting with and immediately got on his phone and started packing up a few of his belongings. I told him we were just catching up, that we had not talked in ten years. He called Rita, told her that I was talking to my ex-boyfriend on the computer and for her to come get him.

I tried to calm him down, but he was not having it. I followed him around telling him that I loved him and did not want to lose our family. I was not doing anything wrong. She got there quick, which indicated that she had been here before, and he was just looking for a way out.

Since he was leaving either way, I went back to the computer and told Wes what had happened. He asked me if I wanted him to come see me. I did, but again I did not. I could use some comfort right now. I felt my family was ripped apart right in front of me, and there was nothing I could do. I told Wes to come, and we could finish catching up.

I prayed to God and asked him why. Why couldn't we just be a happy family? I asked to show Dean how much I wanted us to be a family, but he was not listening to me. Again, I felt cursed or punished and did not know why. Was God there for me, or had he deserted me this time? Did he not want my family to work out?

I got the kids up and ready for school. Luckily, Dean was usually asleep when I got them ready for school, so they were not asking questions. I sent them to the bus stop, called in to work, and took a shower.

A couple of hours later there was a knock at the door. It was Wes. He gave me a hug, and we sat down on the couch and talked. We talked for hours. Before I knew it, the kids were about to be home.

I told Wes he should leave and that I did not want them to be confused. His grandma lived up the road, and he said he would go spend the night with her.

The kids came home from school, and Lacy asked where her dad was. I just said he was working. I was not ready for that yet. I helped them with homework, fixed dinner, and gave them baths. Then I let them watch TV.

The phone rang, and it was Dean. He said that he was staying at a hotel and he wanted the kids the next day. They could go swimming. I said it would be okay.

I called Wes and told him Dean would get the kids tomorrow. I had traded shifts and was working the evening shift, and he could come over after I got off. He thought that would be fine. I told him good night and I would see him then.

I told the kids as they were having breakfast that Mommy and Daddy needed a break from each other for a while and that he was coming to get them and take them swimming. Lacy asked me if we were going to get a divorce. I really did not know how to answer that, so I just said we would try the break first.

Dean got there to pick them up, and he picked up some more of his things too. He did not say anything to me nor me to him. I gave all the kids a kiss and told them not to forget to say their prayers and I would see them the next day.

Wes came to pick me up from work that evening. He had rented a movie. We got to the house, and I heated up the pizza I picked up from the store deli. We had just sat down to eat it when Dean barged in through the door. He grabbed Wes by the neck, and I jumped on his back and told him to go. He was drunk, and the kids were in the car. I went to grab the phone, and he grabbed my arm and put me on the ground.

Somehow, I broke free and ran out the back door. He was chasing me, but I was barefooted and faster. I made it to the neighbor's and asked for his phone. I called the police and reported him drunk driving with my kids in the car. I knew Rita's license plate number and vehicle make and model, so I gave all the information to them.

The next morning I had to go to work. Wes said he would take me to a hotel. I called the police for an update, but they had not arrested him. He did not want me staying here knowing Dean had a key. He would take me to look for an apartment Monday.

Was this what God had wanted? I had prayed for him to send Wes to me. I felt like he was the only one that ever loved me. I thanked God for sending him to save me.

I went to work from the hotel. The kids were supposed to come home today although I really did not know what Dean had planned now. After work I went home, and he dropped the kids off without coming in. Thank goodness, no drama.

After the kids were fed, bathed, had teeth brushed, and prayers were said, I tucked them in. Then I gave Wes a call at his grandma's. He came over, and we talked for a while. We said good night, and I went to bed once he left.

After the kids went to school, we were going to look for an apartment. I had to work the evening shift, and Deana was already watching the kids.

We found a three-bedroom, one-bath apartment two streets over from the trailer house where we now lived. He paid the first and last month's rent on it. All I had to pay was the current-month rent and electric deposit.

That night I went to work and told my manager what my plans were. I also admitted that he was right about the past when he asked me if I was abused. He agreed to help me get out any way he could. I was lucky to have such a great boss. He was going to give me time off with pay to move.

Deana called me to tell me that Dean was at the house taking things. I questioned her about what things he was taking. It was the computer and the big screen TV. That did not bother me, after all those were still being paid on, and I did not have the funds.

The next day while the kids were in school, I was going to have a lot of help and get moved into the apartment. We moved and unpacked one room at a time again. That is best when moving nearby, saves so much time and is so organized. We started early, and by the time the kids got out of school, we were almost done.

There were only two things I wouldn't be able to move out, my father's gun cabinet that he made. It was so heavy, and the apartment was upstairs. I figured it would be safe and Dean wouldn't do anything to it. The other was the waterbed, which was not allowed in an upstairs apartment.

The kids were confused at first. I explained to them that Mom and Dad could not live together anymore. There was too much fighting between us, and that was not fair to them. David blurted loudly, "And Daddy has a girlfriend."

Lana said, "I play the piano at her house and pet her cat." I thought to myself, *Oh my gosh! He's taken the kids to her house.* That reassured me that I was making the right move by getting out.

I introduced them to Wes, my friend, and told them that he was going to be moving into the apartment. Wes had brought his PlayStation. After we ate dinner, he played it with the kids before saying prayers and tucking them in.

CHAPTER FORTY-ONE

Deana and Collin just lived in the next apartment over, which was very convenient. She kept an eye on them for me even though Wes was there with them. That gave them a chance to get to know him.

Wes had a doctor appointment back in his hometown. He would be gone for a couple of days. Deana agreed to watch them, and they could even stay home. Lacy was mature enough to call Deana or knock on the adjoining wall if anything was needed.

I had prayed about it and decided to give Jolie a call. After all she was the only mother that I had ever known. I know you must forgive to be forgiven, and I really missed her.

I knew Richard's number from when I was a child. I just hoped that he had the same one. I nervously asked if she was there. He told me that she was and asked me if I was going to start trouble again. "No, I wanted to ask her to forgive me." I said.

She got on the phone, and I admitted that I had acted in a very immature way and hoped that she could forgive me. I told her that I was sorry that my kids had not gotten to know her and that I would be truly embarrassed had they seen the way I had acted toward her.

"Can you ever forgive?" I asked her.

"Yes," she answered.

I must admit, my heart sure did feel a little lighter.

I also decided I should call Aunt Elsa. The way I had talked to her was wrong. I should have never put them in that position. She answered the phone, and I was nervous. I said, "Aunt Elsa?" She said, "Hello?" I told her it was me and that I had left Dean and apologized for my actions. She always treated me like a daughter, buying clothes and makeup all the time.

I told her that I was filing for divorce next week. I filled her in about what happened and that Wes and I had gotten an apartment.

She was happy I was with Wes; she had always liked him. She accepted my apology and told me to come by and bring the kids to see her and Mamaw. I said I would and that I loved them both.

After a couple of days, Wes came back, and the kids were ready to play the PlayStation again. I could tell they really liked him.

My next day off I had Wes take me to the pawnshop, and I sold my wedding ring. Next, we went to the courthouse, and I filed for divorce. I had Jenna, Dean's ex-girlfriend, to file the paperwork and serve him. Afterward she called me and let me know that he had signed the waiver and was not going to fight me for a hearing. He agreed to the child support amount I was asking for.

I went to see Dean at work. He invited me into his office. Unbelievably, he was truly kind. He actually teared up when he looked at me, saying, "So this is it? We're getting a divorce." I said, "I believe it is for the best." Then he gave me a hug, and we cried together.

I told him where I had moved and gave him the keys to the house. He said he wouldn't feel right living there and that he had gotten an apartment already. I let him know that I had left my dad's gun cabinet and waterbed there. He said he was going to see if Jenna and her husband wanted to rent the home.

The next thing was to tell the kids about the divorce. It should be final in thirty days. They took it better than expected. They knew Rita was living with Dean, and they were glad I had Wes with me and said I wouldn't be lonely when they stayed with their dad.

There was a playground right in front of our apartment for the kids. They were able to play with some of their friends from school, and I could see them from the windows.

I had to meet them when they would get off the bus because if not, they went straight for the playground before even bringing in their backpacks. Getting them to do their homework was tough too. I had to check their backpacks myself to see if there was homework, or they would just say they didn't have any.

When I was working, I would have Deana meet them and check their backpacks. After homework was done, they had an hour to play. Then it was dinner and baths. If Wes was home, they would play the PlayStation for an hour. If not, they would watch TV. Then it was prayers and bedtime.

The divorce was finalized once we had lived in the apartment for about six weeks. I had saved up a little money that gave me a down payment on a used car to get me back and forth to work.

Occasionally, I would notice this man at the store I worked in. He would push an empty grocery cart and follow me around the store. I left work one night, and he was parked across the street at the car wash. When I pulled out, he followed me. This went on a few times. I got home one evening, and he had left a note on my door with his name and number and a message saying that he knew I was divorced.

Then one afternoon, I was getting some change out of the safe for a cashier. When I stood up, the man was at the counter. I quickly shut the safe and closed my thumb in it. Oh, what pain! I had to reopen the safe to get my thumb out.

My thumb was literally flat. I went to the sink and ran cold water on it. I was crying in pain. It was so bad. I went to the back room so the customers wouldn't see me. When I came out, I saw Wes. He asked me what was wrong, and I showed him my thumb. I asked him to drive me to the ER.

When I got in his car, I noticed the back seat was full. He told me that he had another appointment with his doctor out of town and he didn't know when he'd be back.

A doctor saw me right away when we arrived at the ER. I had x-rays taken. I called Dean to see if he could pick up the kids. He was off work that day and said he would be happy to. The doctor came in and said luckily nothing was broken but I might have spliced a nerve or tendon and referred me to an orthopedic.

Afterward, I had Wes take me to the pharmacy to pick up a prescription. Once my prescription was ready, I was happy to go home and rest. I asked Wes if he really had no clue when he might come back. He said he was unsure how long it would be.

When I walked into the apartment, I knew he wasn't coming back at all. I checked the dresser and closet. All his clothes were gone. I felt like I was in high school again when he left with his mom. A deep stab right through my heart. He had hurt me all over again.

I lay on the couch and cried. I asked God, "Why? Why was this happening again? What have I done? Why is happiness not in the future for me?" Then I felt like he answered me. He said, "You prayed for me to bring Wes back into your life. That is what I have done. You were never going to leave a bad situation, and Wes helped to bring you out. His job was complete." Even though it still stung, it was true. I never would have left, and there was no telling what would have happened.

I called the police and told him about that man stalking me. I had saved the note and told them he'd followed me a couple of times. I, being a single parent, was very scared. The officer knew him and said he would go talk to him for me and warn him to stay away from me.

I called Dean and told him what the doctor said about my thumb and that Wes had left. He was really understanding and compassionate. He told me that he would keep the kids for a couple of days so I could take it easy. Then I called my boss and told him what the doctor had said about my thumb and that I would be out for the rest of the week.

CHAPTER FORTY-TWO

I was back to work at the store when I saw Marie. I hadn't talked to her in a while. We never rented movies anymore, and I was usually busy when she came into the store. I told her I had divorced Dean and was living in an apartment. I was shocked when she told me that she lived in the same complex. Her apartment was in the building just behind mine.

She helped with my depression since all I did was go to work and come home. She had an extra computer, which she let me borrow, and gave me her info so I could get online and at least chat with other people. Marie was a great friend who I really needed. She had a gym membership and talked me into going to workout with her three times a week. I was sore at first but was feeling better about myself than I had in an exceptionally long time.

If I was off and the kids were in school, Marie and I would go to the gym, watch movies, and hang out. We became exceptionally good friends. Her daughter, Nicole, and Lacy became good friends as well.

It was getting close to Christmas, and I knew it was going to be a tough one for the kids. It would be the first one since the divorce. I didn't know how I was going to buy their gifts. I was having a hard enough time paying the bills, and Dean wasn't paying child support.

The kids and I decorated the tree and tried to make the apartment have some holiday cheer. I prayed for God to please help me find a way to give the kids a good Christmas.

Eugene stopped by the grocery store while I was working. I had not seen him in a few years. He was living about three hours south and was visiting his family for Christmas. I told him where I was living and to stop by so we could catch up.

A week before Christmas, on a day I just happened to be off, the doorbell rang. By the time I made it to the door, there was no one there, just a couple of big trash bags. I brought them in one at a time. They were heavy. When I looked inside, they were full of toys and clothes for the kids. I broke down in tears and thanked God, for I knew he had provided again.

I went to the dollar store and picked up some tape and wrapping paper. When I got home, I quickly wrapped them all and put them under the tree. I left a couple unwrapped and put them in the trash bag to be from Santa. I called Deana to see if I could hide them at her apartment until Christmas.

Eugene stopped by the apartment as I was getting ready to run the store before the kids came home and grabbed something for dinner. I asked him if he wanted to go with me. We went in his truck since it was already warm. He asked me to go out with him. However, I turned him down as he had done me in high school.

When we got to the checkout, we just happened to be in line behind his mom. She asked the cashier, "Don't they make a cute couple?"

As I laughed, I said, "Trisha, we are just friends."

She smiled and said, "Maybe now, but one of these days. Mother knows best."

I gave her a hug before she left the store. She was so sweet.

When the kids came home from school, they were surprised and happy to see gifts under the tree. Now it felt like Christmas. There were even a few gifts to go in the stockings. I was so happy to see the kids have that joy in their eyes.

Two days later when I was home again, the doorbell rang. This time I opened it and saw a bicycle and another bag. A lady was also standing there. She said she was from the church in town and there was another bag she had to grab. Wow! The kids were really going to have a good Christmas. I was so happy! The lady came back with another bicycle and bag. I helped her get them up the stairs. I gave her a big hug and thanked her. She said that an anonymous donor had donated these things for my kids. I knew it was God's work. "Thank you, God!" I spoke.

I called Deana and asked if I could store a couple of more things. I locked the bicycles in my outdoor storage closet. Then I quickly wrapped the rest. The kids came home to see more gifts, and their eyes were huge and had a joyful spark in them.

Today was their last day of school before the Christmas break. Three more nights and it would be Christmas Eve. I couldn't wait to see their faces on Christmas morning. They would leave at noon to spend Christmas Day with Dean and his family.

After I finally got the kids to go to bed on Christmas Eve, we were having a little Christmas get-together at Deana's apartment. Marie had gotten to know Collin and Deana and came over too. Collin had brothers that were twins, Blake and Jake, and they were there. We played the bad Santa game and had a couple of glasses of wine.

I was taking the first load of stored gifts from their apartment and saw Eugene at my door. I hollered out to him, and he came to give me a hand. I had him go back with me to Deana's and help with the rest of the gifts.

He helped me put the ones together that needed assembling. I was happy he came over because I couldn't have assembled these by myself. I got the bicycles from the storage room and put bows on them. He stayed and visited for a bit.

Time flew by as we were visiting. I had to get to bed because I knew the kids would be up at the crack of dawn eager to open gifts and see what Santa had brought them.

It was Christmas morning, and the kids came running into my room, jumping onto my bed in excitement! Screaming "It's Christmas! Santa came, Mama!" I got up and went into the living room with them. "Look! Lana and I got bicycles!" shouted David.

I had them sit down next to me. "Before we open gifts, I want you all to tell me what Christmas is really meant to celebrate."

They all looked at me with big smiles and said at the same time, "Jesus's birthday! Happy birthday, Jesus!" Then we said a little prayer before they opened the presents.

David asked, "Mama, why did Santa not bring you any presents?" I told him seeing all their smiles was my present.

I let them play with their gifts while I fixed them breakfast and hot chocolate. Afterward, I told them to go put everything in their rooms and get dressed.

Then Lacy helped me pick up all the wrapping paper and put it in a trash bag. She was wearing one of her new outfits, and it looked so cute on her. Lana came into the living room asking for me to help her get dressed. She was wearing a new outfit too. I went to go see what David was doing since I hadn't heard him in a while. He was playing with his new cars and track still in pajamas. I picked him out some clothes and told him he could play after he got dressed until his dad got there.

I really didn't want them to go because it was such a good feeling seeing their smiling faces and how happy they were. I didn't know what I would do after they left.

It was five minutes until noon, and there was a knock at the door. It was Dean coming to pick up the kids. David shouted, "Daddy, check out my new bike! Can I ride it for a few minutes?" Lana wanted to ride hers too. Dean and I helped them down the stairs with their bikes, and they rode them up and down the sidewalk.

Dean asked me, "Have you been working out?"

I replied, "Yes, I have." He told me that he could tell it and to keep it up. I said, "I don't know how I will be able to, Marie moved to California, and I was using her membership."

I told the kids that we had to put the bikes up so they could go with their dad. We grabbed their clothes bags, and I walked them to the car. I told them "Merry Christmas" again and that I loved them. They all gave me tight hugs and thanked me for their presents, gave me kisses, and got in the car. They didn't see it, but I cried as they drove away. It just wasn't going to be Christmas without them.

I called Jolie since we were speaking again and told her "Merry Christmas." Then I got dressed so I could go to Mamaw's house for Christmas lunch.

It was nice to see some family that I hadn't seen in a long time. Perry and I used to fight over who got the leftover chocolate pie Mamaw made. I told him that he had gotten them for years and now it was my turn.

I wanted to get home before dark, and it was starting to snow. I feared driving in rain or snow. I made it home safely. Then Jake and Blake came over.

We played poker, rummy, and other card games as we listened to Christmas music. Then ice started coming down hard. Everyone left before it got too bad. Before I knew it, the power was out, and you could hear limbs falling and hitting the ground.

I grabbed an ice chest and filled it with as many groceries from the freezer and fridge I could then stuck it on the balcony. I also put Dr Peppers and milk outside.

I grabbed as many comforters and blankets as possible and put them on my bed. Then I put on layers of clothes. I climbed in bed under all the blankets to stay warm.

There was a knock at the door. Who could be out on the streets in this? It was Eugene. He asked me if I needed anything. I really could use water, a flashlight, candles, and batteries.

He drove me to the grocery store I supervised. I grabbed the flashlight from under the cash register and a basket. I told him to get what he needed as well. He grabbed a couple of Cokes, water, and batteries.

I made a list of everything we took and left it at the register. I was sure my boss won't mind. I couldn't call to ask; the phones were down too.

Before Eugene took me home, I had him take me by Dean's to check on the kids. They were good. His dad had a fireplace, and they were all huddled in the living room, nice and warm. I gave them all hugs and kisses and told them I would see them as soon as it was safe to come home.

Ice was still coming down as Eugene took me home. He helped me up the stairs with the things from the store. He said that he was going to try to drive back home. I begged him to just stay with his parents until it got better outside. He said he was going in the morning.

I had some charcoal and hamburger meat. I had Eugene get the grill going so we could cook burgers. The least we could do was eat. I was starving. I could eat cereal later I suppose.

After Eugene and I ate, he went back to his parents' house, and I climbed into the bed again to stay as warm as possible. This was going to be the longest boring time of my life!

CHAPTER FORTY-THREE

As it turned out, this was a wintry weather phenomenon unlike any this area had seen in recorded history. It had gotten so cold so fast that trees were literally exploding. Electrical lines never stood a chance. If the falling limbs didn't take them down, the ice buildup would short them out. The damage was so severe it could be a month or more before all utilities were back to normal.

I slept unless I had to use the bathroom. Then I ran back to the bed. The next morning there was a loud knock on the door. It was Rick, a friend from school. He asked me what I was still doing here. I said that I didn't have anywhere to go.

He told me to grab some clothes and come with him, that he had gas. I could take a warm bath and be in a heated home.

That sounded nice, so I grabbed a bag of clothes and got in his nice, warm truck. It was so bright, white, and pretty out here. Just very, very cold.

I asked Rick how he knew that I would be home. He told me that he didn't. He was just taking a drive checking things out and thought that he would go by and check on me.

I knew God had sent him to me. He was a great friend, nothing more. More like the brother I never really had. He had gone by to make sure that his mom was okay, and she didn't live too far from me. He was a good son too. Loved his mom dearly.

Once we made it to his nice and warm house, he showed me where the bathroom was and even started bathwater for me. He said he was going to go fix me a hot meal while I took a bath.

It was so nice to take a hot bath. I lay there soaking in the tub thinking about how our God really takes care of us. He sends angels to us when in need. Sometimes they are family members, friends, or they can even be complete strangers.

I thanked God for sending Rick, my angel, today to take care of me at my time of need. I prayed that he kept my kids warm and fed during this time that I was not able to.

Rick knocked on the bathroom door and asked if I was okay. I told him I was great. He let me know that the food was ready.

I got out of the tub and put on clean clothes. I was able to just put on one layer and still be warm since it was nice and toasty in his home.

He had fixed us a great meal. After we ate, he showed me the guest room so I could get settled in and asked if I'd like a glass of wine. That sounded like a great ending to a nice, warm evening.

After a glass of wine, we told each other good night, and I went and climbed into the comfortable bed in the warm home. When my head hit the pillow, I instantly fell asleep.

I stayed with Rick for some time. After breakfast one morning, we were watching the news. Power companies had sent in help from other states. There were reports that power had been restored in certain areas, and we thought we would go for a drive.

Once we pulled into my apartment complex, I saw my porch light was on. That meant my power was turned back on. Thank you, God!

Rick helped me up the slick stairs, and I thanked him again for coming to my rescue. I went to my bedroom and took all the blankets to the rooms they belonged in and cleaned up the apartment.

After I cleaned up, I called over to Dean's dad's. Dean Sr. answered and told me Dean had left the day before, but the kids were still at his house. I told him I would come pick them up.

Thankfully, the maintenance man had salted the stairs. They were just slushy now. I feared falling and breaking my tailbone again.

I let the car warm up. Then I went to Dean's dad's to get the kids. He just lived two streets over, thank goodness. I still didn't want to drive on these roads. There was a lot of black ice out there.

I left my car running while I went inside to help the kids get their things. I thanked Dean Sr. for keeping them warm for me. He didn't mind. He said he enjoyed their company.

Once home, Lana and David asked if they could ride their bicycles.

"No, it's still too cold," I told them. "You can play with your new toys inside."

Kids! How they can tolerate the cold outdoors is beyond me. I remember loving to play in the snow as a kid and my parents forcing me to come inside. Now you couldn't pay me to stay out there.

The morning after, I had to go back to work. Deana was going to watch the kids. Since I couldn't trust them to stay inside, she was bringing her daughter over to my house. Lacy told Deana that she would babysit Mikayla and she could watch Lana and David.

I really hated going back to work. I had enjoyed the time off but not the circumstances. We had so much to do at work, so at least the day went by quickly. We weren't open yet since we had no frozen or refrigerated foods. We had to throw it all out after we counted it. That way insurance would pay to replace it.

After we threw it all out, we had to clean the freezers and refrigerators. It was a long day no matter how fast it went by, and we were all worn out.

I was glad to get home. I just wanted to lie down and relax. I brought home some bread and told the kids it was going to be peanut butter and jelly sandwiches for dinner. Lacy fixed them for everyone. She enjoyed fixing foods for her sister and brother.

CHAPTER FORTY-FOUR

Marie called to check on us. We had chatted on the computer a little, but it had been a while since the storm, and I had missed hearing from her. She sounded troubled. When I repeatedly questioned if she was okay, she finally said no. She let me know that she only had a few minutes to talk.

Since she moved to California, this man was being terribly controlling of her. She wasn't allowed to talk to friends, she couldn't go anywhere, he blocked her car in the driveway with his truck, she had to give her child support checks to him, and she had to go to bed when he did.

The only way she was able to talk to me was she sent her daughter next door to borrow a phone from the neighbor and had to call me collect. I told her we had to work out a plan to get her home safely.

He had previously said that I could visit after the first of the year. I told Marie to tell him that if I hadn't heard from her and that visit wasn't arranged soon that she knew I would call the police. She agreed. It sounded like a great idea, and we hung up.

I told Collin and Deana what was going on. We decided that since Marie was well known throughout our community that we would start a collection for her around town. Also, I had been chatting online with someone in the same town that she was living in, and he agreed if needed he would go see her.

The next day she called me on a collect call again. She told me that she let him know what we had talked about, and he would let her call me in a couple of days. I told her about the guy I had chatted with and that he would help if needed. She said that would be great. I made her give me the exact physical address, and if I had not heard from her, I would send my friend named Matt over there.

It was New Year's Eve. Dean picked up the kids, and I got ready for work. My job was open and had received one freezer and one refrigerator truck in. It seemed like as fast as we could stock the shelves they became empty.

I had put a collection jar at each of the registers for Marie. They read "Help bring Marie home" and just had a small paragraph saying she was stranded in California. They were collecting quite a bit, which I knew they would because everyone knew and loved her.

A few of us had talked about going into town and celebrating the New Year at the local club after we got off work. Then people started coming into the store saying that it was snowing. It was coming down fast. However, we couldn't see it from the fogged-up windows.

By the time we closed the store, there was at least a foot of snow on the ground. I told everyone they could just come to my apartment and play games if they wanted, that I was not going to town in this snow.

Deana and Collin came over along with Blake and Jake. Another couple, Alyssa and Luke, came over too. I had known Luke since elementary. He was like a brother to me. Deana laid Mikayla down on the couch, and Alyssa almost sat down on her had Jake not stopped her.

We all played Farkle and counted down at the New Year. Everyone had someone to kiss at midnight except me. Oh well, it was just a kiss. We played some more Farkle until the wee hours in the morning and everyone went home. I went to bed since the kids weren't coming home until the next day and the store was closed.

I had to work the early shift on January 2. Dean would take the kids to Deana's. I would pick them up when I got off.

The collection jars for Marie were doing quite well. I went ahead and counted them and bought a money order. I hoped it would be enough to get her home. I was going to mail it to her neighbor's house.

When I got off, I went to the post office and mailed the money order. Then I went to pick up the kids at Deana's, and we went home. There was still too much snow on the ground for the kids to ride their bikes. I told them to come inside for a while and maybe I would let them go outside and play for a little before dark.

As we were walking inside, the phone was ringing. I told Lacy to answer it as I brought in groceries and started to put them away. She was quite a chatterbox on the phone. I could tell it was Marie from what Lacy was saying, so I asked her to finish putting away the groceries and took the phone.

Marie said "Happy New Year" right off the bat. So I knew her boyfriend was home. I asked her if she was okay, and she said yes. Then she said things were crazy at work for him right now and he wouldn't be around to take me sightseeing, so we should wait awhile before I go visit. I told her about the collection and asked if I should get Matt to come over. She agreed. "That sounds like a great idea" were her exact words.

"Let me know when you get the money order, and I will have him come over. I'll track it," I replied.

"Okay, you too. I love you," she said as she hung up.

I was really worried about her. I told Lacy to put on her watch and that she could take Lana and David outside for thirty minutes. They got all bundled up and went outside. I sat a timer on the stove and got online to see if Matt was on. I caught him up on Marie's situation and asked when her neighbor got the money order if he would help her out. He agreed and would go by there tomorrow to meet her and physically check on her.

The timer went off, so I had to go round up the kids. I thanked him and signed off. I went to the door and called for the kids to come inside. I was going to cook them dinner. They came in and turned on the TV. They had to go back to school tomorrow if the roads were clear enough, so I told them we would pretend like they were just in case.

After dinner, I gave the kids a bath and had them pick out their clothes for school. I blow-dried Lacy's and Lana's hair and let them all watch an hour of TV before putting them to bed and saying prayers. When I was leaving the bedroom, Lana called my name, and when I asked what she needed, she replied, "Jimmy did bad things to me at the big house." She was referring to the two-story house we lived in previously.

I asked her, "What kind of things?" She just pointed. I was furious! I trusted him with my kids, and he watched them often when I worked nights at the bar and grill. I let him, his mother, and sister live with us. "Why haven't you told me this before?" I asked her. "He told me not to tell anyone." I told her we would talk more tomorrow. I gave her another kiss and hugged her tightly.

I went to Lacy's room next. I asked her, "Has anyone ever touched you where they shouldn't?" She replied, "No. Why?" I just told her I was curious.

Then I went to my room. I got down on my knees and asked the Lord to give me guidance and show me how to manage the situation. Because I knew right at that moment, I didn't want to manage it appropriately.

Lacy came into my room crying and said, "Mama, I lied." I asked her what she meant. She said, "Jimmy has touched me where he shouldn't." I asked her how many times, and she just told me a lot. I hugged her tightly and told her that I believed her and tomorrow we would go talk to someone about it. She asked me if she could sleep with me, and I told her to climb on in, and we cuddled until we fell asleep.

CHAPTER FORTY-FIVE

It didn't seem like I slept very long when the alarm started beeping. I did not want to get up, but I had to check and see if the kids were having school.

It looked like there wouldn't be school. I called Beth and told her what the girls had told me and that I was calling in to work and calling the police.

I called the owners of the store and told them I would not be in today. Then at eight o'clock I called the police station. An officer picked up the phone, and I told him what my girls had told me. They gave me a lady's number who managed these cases, so I called her next. She set up an appointment for me to bring them up to visit with her that afternoon. I called Beth and told her and asked her if she would go with me. She agreed.

We went to the address the lady had given me that afternoon. She asked if she could talk to each of them alone. I said, "Of course." She then took the girls back one at a time.

When she had finished talking to them, she took all the kids to a toy room and Beth and I to her office. There was a window in her office to the toy room so we could see them.

She started with, "These types of cases where the victims are so young, and we have no physical evidence are very hard to prove in court." At the time their assault would have happened, Lana would have been three and Lacy seven.

She let us know that she would take her reports to the district attorney and they would get back to us.

When we got home, I tried to call Dean to tell him what was going on. Rita answered his phone and said he was back in jail. That didn't surprise me.

I got online, and Matt was on. He asked me to come to California so I could accompany Marie back home. I couldn't take off work long enough, and Dean wasn't around to watch the kids. I would love to but knew I wouldn't be able to.

The day the school was finally opened, I told the kids what time the bus was coming and fixed them all some oatmeal. Then I went to get dressed for work. I gave them all a kiss and told them that I would see them that evening.

The new manager seemed to be catching on quickly. I was glad because I hated training.

After work, I went online when I got home. I saw Matt was on. He had gone by and checked on Marie. He said physically she looked good. However, he could tell that she wasn't mentally. He gave me a phone number and said it was to a cell phone that he had given Marie. He also gave her some money. He said when she got back home that she could send him the phone, but he didn't want her and her daughter on the road alone without a phone.

That evening Marie called. She told me that Matt was nice. I knew God put him in our path to get her back home where she belonged. She said she had to go but as soon as that money order was in she was coming home.

It was Saturday, and I was supposed to be off. The supervisor called me and said the new manager did not show up. I told her to try to call him and give it an hour. If he wasn't in or she hadn't heard from him to call me back.

A few minutes later, the key supervisor called back, and the manager still hadn't come in, nor did he answer her call. This meant that I was going to have to go to work. Probably the next day as well. I told her that I would be in as soon as possible.

I called Beth to see if she could watch the kids. She told me to bring them over. I woke them all up to get dressed and told them that they were going to Grandma's house for the night.

I went to work but only long enough to get done with the manager's work, which was about three hours. Then I went home and got online. Matt was online. I told him that the money order was delivered and that I hadn't heard from Marie. He said unfortunately that he was working out of town but would go by there Monday when he got home.

My alarm went off at nine-thirty. I called the store to see if the hired manager had arrived. He had not, nor had he called. So I got up and got dressed for work.

I got to work and checked on everyone, made sure they all had enough change in their registers. I did the manager's work. Got everyone lined up for side duties. Then I went to Beth's house to pick up the kids.

She asked me to stay for dinner that the kids had been helping her prepare. I told her that Rita said Dean was back in jail. She wasn't surprised either.

After dinner, we all helped clean up, thanked her for the dinner, and went home. The kids needed baths and to get ready for school. I needed to take a shower and get ready for another day's work.

The next morning after I got to work, I called the owner and let him know that the new hire was a no call no show for three days. I told him I was off both days and had to come in. He told me to do the same today and he would have another manager for me to train tomorrow.

I went home and got online and saw Matt was on. I asked him if he had talked to Marie. He had gone by there but thought the boyfriend might have been there, so he didn't stop.

A couple of hours later Marie called. He had gone to work. She had packed and hid some things and was packing some more. She called Matt's friend to come pull the boyfriend's truck out of the way.

She would call me when she got on the road on her way back home. I couldn't wait to give her a big hug. I had missed her so much.

The next morning I went to work, and not long after, the owner came in with another manager for me to train. I hoped he was a fast learner too.

He caught on quickly. After three days, I felt that he was ready for his own shift. I was going to get a full day off. It had been a while since that had happened.

Marie called me when I got home. In about four hours she would be back. She and her daughter were going to stay with me until she could get back on her feet.

The new manager had worked for two weeks when he put in his notice. I called the owner to let him know. He told me to go ahead and take his front door keys and that he didn't want him there without me.

I asked him if he would just promote me to store manager rather than have me keep training one. Obviously, I had proven that I can do it multiple times. His response was, "Legally we cannot have this conversation, but a woman will never be a store manager for me."

I said, "Well, you'd better send someone else to do all of your training and run the store until then because I quit!" I left my keys in the desk drawer and told everyone to have a wonderful day as I walked out.

I had never been so mad at an employer and never just walked out on a job. On my way home I prayed for the Lord to please send me another job to be able to support my kids.

CHAPTER FORTY-SIX

When I got home, I called Mr. and Mrs. Powers, the owners of the burger place that Dean managed. They owned a few different stores. It just so happened that their sandwich and gas store was needing a manager. They asked me to come to the store the following day to speak with them.

After I hung up with them, the phone rang. It was the social worker that I had taken the girls to see. Unfortunately, she said the case would not go to court. The best thing I could do was get them into counseling. They provided that at her office. We made an appointment for them.

Marie and her daughter, Nicole, made it back safely. It was good to see her face, and it felt awesome to hug her neck. Nicole was happy to be back in town too. She called one of her friends to let her know that she was back and made plans to go to her house.

Marie and I talked for a couple of hours. She was going to help me with the kids until she found a job and got back on her feet. The kids were excited to see her when they got home. We helped the kids with homework and fixed dinner. I let them watch TV while we cleaned up the kitchen, gave them baths, said prayers, and put them to bed.

I had to get up early to go meet Mr. and Mrs. Powers. Marie got up with me and fixed the kids' breakfast. I had picked out their clothes the night before, so they all got dressed and brushed their teeth. I was getting ready to leave too.

I told Marie to take it easy today since she had such a long day yesterday. I shouldn't be long, and we could talk some more.

I didn't see Mr. Powers when I arrived, but Mrs. Powers was behind the counter at the sandwich shop. I let her know that I was there, and she said to have a seat and she would be right with me.

We talked a little about my experience, and she asked me if I had anything to do with Dean. When I told her that I didn't, she let me know that they were planning to take him to court for theft. For some reason, that didn't shock me. I let her know that he was already in jail.

She asked if I could start the next day. I told her the sooner, the better. We agreed I would work Tuesdays through Saturdays, nine o'clock in the morning until five o'clock, and have Sundays and Mondays off.

I really thought I would like the schedule. I could get the kids off to school myself. Marie would be here in the afternoons to get them off the bus. I would have Sundays off with them or to go out on Saturday nights when Beth or Leena had the kids. I knew since Marie was back that she would want to go out some now.

While Marie cooked dinner, I made sure the kids had their homework finished, picked out their clothes for tomorrow, and let them play outside for an hour.

I called the kids in once it was ready. I sent them to wash their hands, and we all sat down at the table. I prayed, thanking God for sending Marie home safely and for this wonderful meal she had prepared for us, asking for him to keep us all safe.

It was my first day at my new job, and I was incredibly nervous. The Powers were ridiculously hard to work for. When I arrived, she was there waiting for me. She introduced me to the staff as their new store manager and told them to not give me a tough time. She gave me keys and a shirt. Then she left me in charge.

It had been years since I had worked in a sandwich shop, but I was quite sure it would come back to me quickly. The gas registers were on the same software we used at the grocery store, self-explanatory.

The first part of the day, which included the lunch rush, went by easy. Now we would see how the shift change went. The next crew that came in was introduced to me by the morning shift. Before I left for the day, I asked everyone if they needed anything and then wished them a good night.

I went home, and we all shared our day. Marie had already helped with homework and picked out clothes for tomorrow. It looked like our little system was working out nicely. All three of my kids loved Marie and Nicole. Lacy and Nicole were close. I loved having them around also.

It was the day to take the girls to their appointment. Once we arrived, the counselor took them back one at a time and visited with them. When both visits were complete, she sent them to the toy room and asked me to come into her office. She told me that she thought they would benefit from having a few more visits.

This routine went on for a couple of months. Then Marie told me that she thought it was time for her to find her own place. I understood, but I didn't want her to go. I felt like everyone always had to leave me.

She said that it would still be another month or so, and she had to start with a job first. She was going to search on the computer for work, and I would bring her a newspaper home to check the classifieds.

Leena was going to watch the kids this weekend. Marie and I were going to go out to the club. As soon as Leena picked up the kids, we got ready. We went to the club and saw people that we have not seen in forever. It was packed in there, and that gave me anxiety.

We asked if a couple of people wanted to come back to the apartment and hang out with us. Jake and Blake, of course, wanted to come hang out with us.

We made it back to the apartment. Alyssa and Luke were there waiting for us. When we got inside, I called Deana to see if she and Collin wanted to come over too. She said that they would. Her mom was watching Mikayla, and they really didn't have plans.

It was a full house, and we were having a fun time. Blake and Jake brought beer. I had brought home some wine. Alyssa and Luke brought over some vodka. I admitted that I did not drink much, but I considered that night to be a special night.

I took everyone's keys upon arrival. They would only get them back if I believed that they were sober enough to drive. We took the coffee table out of the living room to make enough room for dancing. Some people played card games. Then we thought charades would be fun. I had more fun than I had in a while. Marie thought so too. Maybe we could do this again before she left.

CHAPTER FORTY-SEVEN

A couple of months had passed, and Marie found a job at a hotel in a couple of towns over that provided her with a furnished apartment. I couldn't blame her for accepting it. I was sad that she was leaving, but happy for her.

Dean hadn't paid child support at all, and I was getting behind on my bills. One morning I went out to get in my car to go to work and it was gone. I only owed $350 on it, and it would be paid off. I called the dealership, and they said that I had to pay it in full to get it back.

I called Mrs. Powers and told her what was going on to see if they would give me an advance. She said they would, and I had to pay back $100 a paycheck.

I also received an eviction notice. I went to the office at the apartments and showed them my tax return that I had just filed. I told them that I would pay six months' rent once I received my refund. They agreed with that. The only bills that were caught up were the internet and phone.

This would be my first time to get a tax return as single with dependents. I was looking at getting back over $5,000. The best part was I wouldn't have someone telling me how we were spending it.

I had Deana take me to the Powers' primary office to get an advanced check. Then to the bank and back to the dealership. I thanked her then got in my car and drove to H&R Block. When I got there, the agent went to get my chart. She said, "Unfortunately, it looks like you had back taxes due because Dean didn't file a W-2 last year." I asked her what that meant, and she told me that they took $4,400 from my check.

"No!" I really needed that check. Now we were going to get evicted for sure. I took the check and paperwork from her and went to the bank.

I cashed the check and drove to the apartments. Now I had to tell the landlord.

I went inside and called Marie first. She said her friend had a house she was selling, and I could probably get it. She gave me the number of the realtor to call.

I asked Deana if she could get the kids for me so that the realtor could meet me at the house in thirty minutes. I assured her that I shouldn't be long. I drove to the address that he gave me. From the outside it didn't look like much, so I didn't get my hopes up.

Once he arrived, we went inside. It looked a lot nicer and bigger inside. There were hardwood floors. Every wall was freshly painted. There were four bedrooms. The front one had a built-in curio. One was small, but it could be a toy room. The kitchen didn't have much counter space but was big enough for an island. A bar separated it from the dining room. It also had a carport, which I never had.

I would receive $1,500 at closing, and the payments were only $275 a month. I could manage that. I asked him when we could move in, and he said by the end of the week. Sunday was my off day and would work perfectly for me.

Between now and Sunday, I brought boxes home for the kids to pack their rooms. I told them to go through their stuff and throw away everything that was broken and make a pile of stuff to donate. I asked around at work if anyone had a truck and could help me, and I got several volunteers.

I put Lacy and Lana in the front room, and David wanted the smaller bedroom. He said it only needed a bed and a dresser and that the other room had more room for their toys. I took the very back room. It only had one bathroom, but that was all we had in the apartment, and we made it work.

We had only been here a couple of weeks when the bathtub and sinks started backing up and really stunk. I had to call a plumber out to snake the line, and he said there were too many roots in the pipes, and they were old. I couldn't let my kids stay here.

I called Beth and told her what was going on, and she came to pick up the kids. I really didn't know what I was going to do. I got down on my knees and prayed.

"Dear Heavenly Father, forgive me for not praying to you and giving you thanks like I should have. Please light a path for me and give me directions on where to go from here."

I got into bed. I didn't know what to do or where to go. I prayed to God for help. "Heavenly Father, forgive me for my sins. What do I do, Lord? Where do I go from here? Please send me a message or a sign. I am stuck and feel like I am sinking. I need your help. Please rescue me and help me to provide for my children."

Suddenly it was clear to me. As a teenager I always wanted to join the military in the back of my mind. At my current age, the only branch that would accept me was the army. I went to see a recruiter. He told me since I was a single mom that I would have to give temporary custody to someone. Dean was in jail again. Beth didn't need to watch them full-time. I would ask Leena.

I went over to Leena's and told her about my plan. I told her that I needed a fresh start for me and the kids. I still had to take the ASVAB test before any confirmation was made in my plans. Leena agreed to keep the kids until Dean got out of jail. I went to Beth's to see the kids and tell her about my plans. It would be a way for the kids to see more of the world. Plus I would be financially stable on my own and not have to rely on food stamps or child support I wasn't even getting.

The kids were staying the night with Beth again. I gave them all a hug and kiss and told them I would come see them tomorrow. Their school was across the street from her house, which was very convenient. We wouldn't say anything to them until we knew for sure what the plan would be.

I called the recruiter and told him that I had planned to give their aunt temporary custody. He picked a day for me to take an ASVAB practice test first. After that was taken, we could go from there.

I stopped by the Powers' primary office to let them know I had decided to enlist in the army and I would have to quit working for them, but I had the money I owed them for the car. Mrs. Powers told me to keep the money, and she totally understood and appreciated that I wanted to serve our country.

I went back to Beth's after she got off work and told her what the recruiter said. She asked me to stay and eat dinner with the kids. I helped them with their homework when they got home while Beth fixed dinner.

Beth's tacos were the best! No matter how hard I tried I could never get them to taste like hers. I gave the kids a bath and helped Beth clean up the kitchen before I said prayers with the kids and tucked them in.

I went back to the stinky house and wondered if it was good for me to be in the house in this shape. I got ready for bed and closed my bedroom door. I also put a couple of towels under the door just to be on the safe side. Tomorrow was the day I would take the practice test. I prayed for God to give me the answers I needed to pass it.

CHAPTER FORTY-EIGHT

I woke up and got dressed to go to the recruiter's office to take the test. I was so nervous. I always had test anxiety before any test I take.

Once I got to the recruiter's office, he took me to a quiet room and gave me my paperwork that I needed to complete before the test. It took a while to complete, but I let him know I was finished with that part. Then he made copies of my birth certificate, driver's license, divorce decree, and social security card.

Next, he gave me the practice test. It took me about an hour and a half to do. He said I should hear back from him in a couple of days.

Instead of going home, I went over to Mamaw's to see if I could take a bath. I told her what had been going on and what my plans were. She thought it would be a terrific way for the kids to travel to various places and see new things as well as meet new friends. She asked me to stay the night there.

I called the kids and told them where I was and that I would see them the next day. Then I told Beth it would be a couple of days before I knew anything.

I went back to the house the next morning. I called the city to see if they would snake their part of the line and see if that made a difference. Shockingly it did! I put the draining hose for the washing machine out the window. I figured it would be less water to drain through the pipes.

I scrubbed, bleached the tub, and washed it out. The final test would be flushing the toilet. Nothing backed up. A guy from the city told me to get copper sulfate and flush it in the toilet and it would kill some of the smaller roots in the pipes. I prayed, "Dear God, please let this work."

Nothing backed up, thank goodness. Now I had to shower off and go see the kids. They were happy to see me. I told Beth I think I had temporarily fixed the sewer issue and I could take the kids home with me for the night to give her a break. I appreciated her help more than she would ever know.

I let the kids play or watch TV for an hour. Then they had to go to bed. Lana and David went to the toy room to play. I told Lacy that I wanted to talk to her. We talked about the chance that I would join the army. She was sad about it and didn't want to leave her family or friends. I understood that and told her that she would get to visit them many times a year. She felt better about it by the end of our conversation. I asked her not to say anything to Lana or David yet, that I wanted to know for sure first. The hour was up, so we said our prayers, and I tucked the kids into bed and said good night.

The recruiter called and said everything looked great and I needed to come in and take the real ASVAB test. I was going to get the kids off on the bus and head that way. It was beginning to look as if I was joining the military.

When I arrived at the recruiting office I was directed to the back. The recruiter sent me into the testing room, started the clock, and had me begin. Oh, the anxiety was taking over. I was trembling all over.

I finished before the timer went off and opened the door. The recruiter looked over at me and motioned for me to come to him. I needed a physical before joining and of course a drug test.

I went to the address he sent me to. They performed a physical examination and collected a urine sample. The physician said they would have the urine culture back tomorrow, but I had passed the physical examination.

I went home and prayed that I did well on the ASVAB then everything else looked good to go for the military. I had the paperwork giving Leena temporary custody of the children until I completed training.

The next morning the recruiter called and said I was clear, that I had passed my ASVAB test and would be shipping out in three weeks. I had to go to the office, get sworn in, and sign my paperwork.

I had a lot to do before I was shipped out. I would be taking basic training in Fort Jackson South Carolina. I needed to get in touch with Mr. Hatridge about the house and see if I needed to move the belongings out. It would more than likely be safer in storage.

Also, I wanted to say goodbye to all my good friends. I had to explain what I was doing to the kids and hope they didn't think I was abandoning them.

I called Mr. Hatridge and told him of my plans to join the army. Luckily, he had been in the military as well and congratulated my efforts to serve our country. He said if I just moved my things out, he would find another buyer.

I went to Rhonda's house, a friend from the alternative school, to tell her goodbye. She and her family were moving as well. They were going to try their luck living on the beach in South Texas.

I went to Anna's house and spent a night with her before I was to leave. She thought I was crazy for joining the military. I thought it would be good for me to gain some independence and allow the kids to see other parts of the world. I was enlisting for eight years.

I called Jake, Blake, Collin, and Michael and asked them to help me put my items in storage. Then I took what the kids would need to Leena's while they were staying there. I would be gone for about eighteen weeks total. Hopefully, I would get to come home to visit before I had to go to AIT training.

We got everything packed up in storage and the kids all settled in over at Leena's. I took the kids with me to Mamaw's for an overnight visit before I was to leave. She and Aunt Elsa were proud of me and hoped it all worked out for the best.

The next night the kids and I stayed with Marie and Nicole. We had a lot of fun playing games and watching movies. She cooked her famous chicken parmesan. It was the kids' and my favorite dish of hers. We went to bed early because I had to take the kids to Leena's, and Marie was going to drive me out of town to catch a plane to basic training.

I took the kids to Leena's the next morning. Saying goodbye was harder than I thought it would be, not really knowing when I would see them again or when I could talk to them on the phone. I tried hard not to cry in front of them although a tear or two did manage to fall. I gave them all kisses, long, tight hugs, and said our goodbyes.

Marie was meeting me at Leena's boyfriend Larry's car repair shop. He was going to let me keep it there while I was gone. Marie was driving me to the airport, which was about an hour and a half away. I was feeling incredibly nervous. Did I make the right decision? There was no turning back now. I had already sworn in.

I said my goodbyes to my dear sweet friend Marie. I told her I would be a soldier the next time we see each other. She just laughed and said, "You are crazy! I can't believe you are going into the army." As I walked away, I smiled and said, "Well, believe it, here I go."

Once the plane landed in Columbia, the new recruits were directed to a bus that took us to the base. It was four o'clock in the morning upon arrival. I was exhausted!

We were directed to an outdoor awning that covered bleachers. Here we were assigned our platoons and barracks. We were lined up and given a large duffel bag to pick up our battle dress uniforms (BDUs), boots, and physical training uniforms (PTUs).

Next, we went through another physical examination. Blood was drawn, and we were told to stand barefoot on a glass block. That would tell them what type of running shoes were best suited for our feet. They gave us a ticket to give to a sergeant, and they gave us our shoes.

When we had everything we needed, we were escorted to our barracks to put our things away and dress in our PTUs. We were to meet back outside of our barracks once we were dressed.

It was here we were told the restrooms were called latrines and we always had to have a friend with us when we went anywhere on base. One walked behind the other. If we came face-to-face with a drill sergeant along our route, we stopped, stood in parade rest, and the person in front would say, "Trained to fight, Drill Sergeant, trained to fight." We would remain in parade rest until the drill sergeant would say, "Carry on, soldier, carry on."

Basic training would last nine weeks. It was two weeks before I got to call the kids. I missed them so much. If we wanted to go, worship services were held on Sundays. I always went to them.

They never let us sleep for more than four hours at a time and were constantly yelling for us to hydrate. (Drink from our canteen, which we must always have on us.)

When going to any meals in the Chow Hall, you waited in an exceptionally long single-file line, and once you had your tray and drink, you had fifteen minutes to eat it.

I always seemed to end up on gate duty. That required me to wear BDUs and check anyone's IDs before opening the gate and announcing on radio their name, rank, and destination. Also required knowing who to salute or call sir or ma'am.

The physical training was harsh and usually about six hours' long a day. I was so glad I worked out every day before I shipped off after being recruited. If not, I would not have been able to last throughout the total hours of training.

When I received my orders, I found out my military occupational specialty (MOS). I was assigned 92A, or what's known as a quartermaster. That advanced individual training (AIT) would be in Fort Lee Virginia for about ten and a half weeks long.

Once I completed that training, the kids could come live with me to Fort Campbell Kentucky where I was to be stationed for two years. Then I would receive new orders.

I called Leena's to let the kids know what my orders were, only to find out that Dean had been released from jail and they were staying with him. So I called them over there and gave them the news. They were both excited and sad to leave their family.

Sadly, the AIT never took place, nor did going to Fort Campbell. Two weeks before graduation, when we were taking our physical training test, I fell and tore my anterior cruciate ligament (ACL) in my knee. I prayed that God would give me quick healing so I could get back home soon.

I had to remain on base for surgery and physical therapy for a month before being discharged. I met a staff sergeant who was also in physical therapy for his neck. His name was Doug, and he was from Upstate New York. We talked a lot and really got to know each other. He was single with four children back home. We shared stories of our kids with one another.

While on crutches, I would work the desk in the officer's office. I was called in and received my discharge papers. I was going home and could see my kids. I called and told them I would be home soon, and we prayed for a safe return. I would have one more day of physical therapy and go back home the next day. Doug asked me to visit him in New York after he was discharged. I was going to be living with Marie, so I gave him her number and told him to call me.

CHAPTER FORTY-NINE

I was having Marie pick me up at the airport since I was going to be living with her. Once onboard the plane, I prayed to thank the Lord for sending me home and that we would arrive safely.

I was so happy to see Marie. I gave her a big hug. Then she teased me for all the weight I had gained. Since I worked in the office after I hurt my knee, I was unable to exercise and did a lot of sitting, which really caused a huge weight gain.

On the way to Marie's, I told her that I might go visit someone in Upstate New York when he got discharged. I told her all about Doug and his kids. She said it sounded like a great idea to see some new parts of the country.

We made it to her house safely, and I got settled in before I called the kids and let them know that I had made it back. They were so happy and couldn't wait to see me the next day. I would give them a call before bed. We said our prayers and good nights.

Marie had fixed a nice dinner for my homecoming. We said grace and enjoyed our meal. I shared how the army had taught me some independence and self-discipline. I was thankful for the experience but happy that it was over.

I had received an honorable discharge since I was injured and a severance pay now that I could not continue due to my injury. I would be able to help Marie with her bills until I figured out what I would do next.

The next morning, Marie drove me to my car. I was going to pick the kids up and bring them with me to Marie's for a few nights. They were out of school for the summer, so they could stay more than two nights.

Lacy would sleep with Nicole, Lana on the couch and David with me. That arrangement was fine with them, especially David. He was a mama's boy.

We played card games, told jokes, and laughed a lot. It was so good to see their faces light up and hear them laughing. We ordered pizza for dinner and watched a movie.

After that, everyone was ready to go to bed. We all said our nightly prayers, and I tucked Lana in. Lacy went to bed with Nicole and David, and I went to sleep quickly.

The next day Doug called for me. I kept our conversation short so I could spend my time with the kids. He had gotten his discharge papers and would be going home to New York the next day. I told him to give me a call in a few days.

The kids, Marie, and I played games again and had grilled hamburgers that night. We also made a little fire and had smores. I was glad that they were having an enjoyable time.

They ended up staying four nights total before I took them back to Dean's house. They were happy to see their dad but sad to see me go too. I cried a little on my way home. I asked God once again to light the path to lead me in the right direction.

Doug called and let me know that he had made it back home. We talked on the phone for hours. Then we got on the computer and chatted so that we could share pictures of the kids.

I had planned to go to the travel company the next day to price plane tickets to go visit him in New York. Since he had just gotten back home, he was staying with his mom but assured me that her house was big, and she didn't mind if I came for a visit.

After we ended our chat, I went to talk to Marie about my plans. She was excited for me and wished that she could go too. She had always wanted to visit New York.

The following day I went to the travel company and got an excellent rate to fly into the LaGuardia airport. I went back to Marie's and called Doug to see if the dates were good with him. The dates were perfect for him, so it looked like I was leaving in a week to spend two weeks there.

I called Dean and filled him in as well as made plans for me to have the kids for a few nights before I flew out. I asked him not to tell them that I wanted to when they were staying with me.

The kids came for four nights, and I let them know during their stay that I was going to New York for two weeks to visit a friend that I had met in the army. I told them that I would call them every night so we could say our prayers before bed.

CHAPTER FIFTY

The day had come, and I was on my way to New York. It was dark when I had landed, and the lights from the city were so bright and pretty. I got off the plane and met Doug at the baggage claim area.

He greeted me with a big hug. It was the first time for us to see each other in civilian clothing, which was kind of strange. After we got my bag, we went to the parking lot and got in his car.

He said it was about a three-hour drive from the airport to the house, so I should get comfortable. I was tired from the long day, so as soon as I laid my seat back, I dozed off.

It didn't seem long when he woke me to say we were almost there. I sat up in my seat to look out the window. All I saw was total darkness. A few minutes later, we pulled into a driveway to an exceptionally large home.

He grabbed my bag and told me to come on in and he'd show me around. We entered through a large kitchen. I could tell it was an old but genuinely charming home. It was then he introduced me to his mother, Jan. She seemed quite nice as she greeted me.

He showed me to my room, which was nice. I also had my own bathroom. After I got settled in and took a shower, I met him downstairs in the living room. He asked if I wanted to watch a movie, but I knew I would fall asleep. I thought it was best if I turned in for the night. I would meet his sons the next day. I called the kids to let them know I had made it safely. We said our prayers and good night.

Jan had fixed us a nice breakfast the next morning. We all sat down at the table where she said grace before we ate. That gave me a good feeling about his upbringing. After breakfast, I helped Jan with the dishes as he went to pick up his sons.

It wasn't very long, and he was back with them. His oldest ran inside straight to me and gave me a hug as he introduced himself to me. His name was Darren. Then Doug came in carrying the other boy. He was small at only two years old. Doug said, "DJ is a little shyer than Darren." He told DJ to tell me hi, but he only turned his head away from me.

He told the boys that we were going to the park and fishing, asked them if they wanted to show me around the town. They said yes with much excitement. Jan had packed us lunch in a picnic basket and gave us a blanket to lay out on the ground.

The fishing at the park was a catch and release, but I could tell the boys enjoyed it very much. Darren was only a year younger than David, and I thought they would get along great. When I told Darren about him, he asked when he could meet him. I told him I would call David tonight and they could talk on the phone. He loved that idea and couldn't wait.

We ate our lunch that Jan had made for us, which was incredibly good. I could tell she liked to cook and was quite good at it. DJ warmed up to me during lunch. In fact, he asked me if I wanted to go see the deer with him.

After we ate, DJ grabbed my hand and said, "Come with me. I will show you. They are right this way." He led me to a huge chain link fenced area that had several deer inside. Once Doug joined us, he said they were rescued deer that had been injured as fawns. They wouldn't be able to live in the wild now as they were hand-fed.

We spent some time at the park to let the boys play. Then as it began to get dark, we headed back to the house. Wouldn't you know it, Jan had the table all set and dinner ready for us as we entered. We went to wash up and all met at the dinner table. This time Jan asked if I would like to say grace. I was happy to do it.

"Father, thank you for this wonderful day that you have given us to have in the beauty you created surrounding us. I want to thank you for giving me this opportunity to meet this wonderful family. Thank you for this food we are about to receive and bless the hands that prepared it. Please keep my children safe and happy and keep us all well. In Jesus's name, amen."

After dinner, I told Darren I was about to call David and my daughters. If he would give me a minute to talk to them, I would let him speak to David. Doug was helping his mother clean up the kitchen. I thought, *What a great man.*

I got in touch with the kids and told them about our day. Then I told

David that Darren wanted to talk to him, so I put him on the phone. Darren was asking him all kinds of questions. Then I heard him ask, "When are you coming to see us?" I asked Darren to let me talk to him now. Then David was asking the same thing. I just answered him by saying, "We will have to see." We said our prayers and hung up.

The next morning we all got ready for church. It was a smaller church than I had imagined, but I was glad. I like small churches, which was where I feel most comfortable. When the very touching service was over, we went out to eat lunch at Friendly's. I had never eaten at one before. Their food was good. Even the ice cream was some of the best I had ever had.

I spoke to my kids every night, and we said our prayers. Then on my sixth night I finally got to meet Doug's daughters. They seemed nice and were very pretty. His oldest daughter, River, was only about six months younger than Lacy. His younger daughter, Erica, was a year older than Lana.

The boys had gone home, and the girls were only staying one night. The four of us played rummy for hours before I noticed the time and needed to make my nightly call to the kids.

While I was on the phone, River asked Doug, "So is she your girlfriend?" Doug answered, "No, we're just friends. We met in the army." Then River said, "But you like her more than just a friend, huh?" He said, "I don't know." Then Erica started singing, "Dad's got a crush." I could tell he was embarrassed and said, "Be quiet, Erica."

I only had three more nights left when Doug told me he didn't want me to leave. He had been a perfect gentleman the entire stay. Hadn't made a single move on me. It was just like we were friends until this night.

We were outside on the porch listening to the river close by and looking at the stars when he asked if I was cold. "A little bit," I replied. He came up behind me and wrapped his arms around me. Then he kissed me on the neck. I was shocked and jumped a little. He apologized for his action and said that was out of line.

I turned around and kissed him back. I told him that I could tell he was a good man and felt he was put in my life for a reason. As for our kids, they would all have a friend close to their age except for DJ. I thought that was neat.

He asked if I was interested in moving up here. I knew it was something that I was going to have to talk to the kids about. I had been here nine nights, and he hadn't made an advancement on me. I thought he didn't like me for more than just a friend.

I went in and called the kids. I talked to them about how we were supposed to move if I would have been able to stay in the army and asked how they would feel about moving to New York.

A couple of days later, instead of me flying back home, Doug and I drove his mom's Jeep Cherokee to Texas to pick up a U-Haul, my things in storage, and the kids. I had prayed about it and felt like this was a move God wanted me to do.

After we made it into town, we stopped by Marie's. We were going to stay here for a couple of nights before we drove back. She said she liked Doug and he seemed nice.

The next night the kids stayed here with us so we could leave out early. We had the U-Haul ready to go. Only Lacy didn't want to go, so she stayed with her dad. Lana and David would go with us.

Before we left, I got down on my knees in the bedroom and prayed. I asked God to put a bubble around us to protect us on this trip back. It was going to be tough, especially with the kids. They were only seven and eight. I asked him to give us patience on the trip with the kids because they had never traveled so far. I also thanked him for allowing us to arrive here safely.

We loaded up the kids and their belongings, said our goodbyes to Marie, and got on the road. We would have to drive slower with towing a U-Haul than we did on the way down.

Doug held my hand as we pulled out of Marie's driveway, waving to her as we left. I never thought a visit to Upstate New York would turn into a move.

While it was daylight, we played the alphabet game with the kids along the trip to help time go by faster. It's where you find a word on a sign or license plate that begins with the next letter in the alphabet until you make it all the way through.

We stopped a few times to stretch, get gas, use the bathroom, or get something to eat. Once it got dark, the kids slept the rest of the trip.

It was late when we got back. I let them both sleep with me and figured the next day we would show them around the big house and get them settled in a room.

We got into bed and said our prayers, thanking God for getting us safely here. I asked him to help me find a job and make it easy on the kids to get settled in. We also thanked him for the beautiful scenery along the way.

The next morning the kids got to meet Jan and have some of her wonderful cooking. I showed them around the big, nice house. He suggested for David to sleep in Darren and DJ's room and Lana could sleep with me.

Doug went to pick the boys up. He knew Darren was excited to meet David, and we knew they would hit it off instantly as they did. He also got Erica to come over and meet Lana. They got along and slept in the second guest room.

Staying here would only be temporary. Then we would find a place after I got a job. Doug had a job at a retirement community as a maintenance man. Jan was the manager. She said she could get me on there part-time as a custodian until I found work. Also, the kids could come with me. I took her up on the offer. I thought it would be an effective way to meet people.

I had to get the kids enrolled in school. They had been going to work with me until it started. I hadn't really looked for another job yet. I wanted us to move and the kids get into school first.

CHAPTER FIFTY-ONE

The kids started school, so I was on the job hunt. I filled my first application out at the local pharmacy, and the store manager, Mary Ann, wanted to interview me on the spot. She liked what she read on my resume, and we clicked right away. She asked if I could start the following Monday. I liked what she had to offer me, including all the benefits, and accepted the offer.

We found a nice triplex on a large plot of land, which the landlord cared for. It was on a foothill of a mountain with a beautiful view. The one we looked at took up the whole second floor. It had two average-size bedrooms and a large one. The kitchen was small, and it only had one bathroom, but we could make it work. There was also a little nook by the stairs that would work for an eating area.

Since we had Doug's boys every other weekend, we gave them the biggest bedroom. We put bunk beds in there, and they had plenty of playing room. Lana took the room beside theirs, and we took the one by the stairs. Our entryway was downstairs along with the washer and dryer.

The driveway was exceedingly long and from the road all uphill and crossed over a creek. Doug said we might have trouble once it snowed making it up to the house. The landlord said he would try to do his best to keep it plowed for us. There was a young couple that lived below us with two small children. The third two-bed apartment was above the garage and empty at the time.

The kids didn't mind walking to the bus stop at the end of the driveway. It was the walking up that they dreaded, especially with band instruments. I could already see that as an issue if it snowed.

Other than that, we loved it! The privacy and the wildlife were amazing. The landlord did warn us not to let the kids outside alone or where we couldn't see them because a mama bear would come around with three cubs. The kids got excited when they heard that and wanted to see them. We all warned how dangerous she would be as she protected them.

We paid our first and last month's rent and moved in. Doug put all the beds together. We let Lana have my bedroom suite that Marie had given me. We took Doug's bed, which was amazingly comfortable.

We finally got settled in, and everyone got their baths and ready for bed. The kids had school, and I would have my first day at work the next day. We said prayers as we thanked God for giving us this beautiful roof over our heads. I gave them kisses and tucked them in.

I sold my car back home, so for now we only had one vehicle. Doug and I took the kids to the end of the driveway and waited for the bus. Then he took me to the pharmacy, which was only a block from the retirement community, so that was convenient.

I nervously went in for my first day. Mary Ann gave me some paperwork to complete and a work smock. Once I completed the paperwork, she gave me a tour and introduced me to everyone. An older gentleman trained me on the register and said we had to do a cigarette count every shift.

After being on the register for half of the shift, Mary Ann had a female employee train me on the back stock and facing the shelves. She also told me if there was ever a slow time to always face the shelves.

Before I knew it my shift was over, and it was time to go. I could tell that I was really going to like this job. Doug had already gone home, and the kids were with him when he picked me up. He was always going to be able to get off in time to be there when they got home.

We made it home, and Doug already had a roast in the Crock-Pot for dinner. We sat down, and I asked David to say grace. His favorite thing he liked to say was, "God is great. God is good. Let us thank him for our food, amen."

After dinner, David and Lana went to their rooms to play. I cleaned up the kitchen, gave the kids a bath, and took a shower. After that, it was pretty much bedtime, and we would do it all over again tomorrow.

CHAPTER FIFTY-TWO

It had been a couple of months since we moved in. The kids were doing well in school. Darren and DJ seemed to love coming over every other weekend. David and Darren were becoming very close. Darren even came every weekend sometimes.

Erica came to stay every now and then. She and Lana got along well too. River didn't come over very often. She was into sports, and her friends lived close to her mom's house.

We called Lacy and spoke to her often. Every few times I tried to talk her into moving up here with us, but she always declined. I also called Anna and spoke to her often. She was expecting another baby in January.

I hadn't been at the pharmacy long when Mary Ann transferred to another store. We got a new manager named Brian. He was nice to work for. He promoted me to key supervisor not long after he started.

There was a couple with a small daughter moving in above the garage. I was off that morning when I noticed the woman was searching for something in the trailer that was loaded with their things. I went outside to introduce myself and see if there was something I could help her with. She said her name was Rachelle and she was looking for her coffee maker. I invited her up to my place and told her that I would make her some. Her husband's name was Brad, and they had a daughter that was DJ's age named Ciara. Now all the kids could have a friend!

Rachelle and I became the best of friends. If I was off and Doug was working and the kids at school, you could find me at her house.

We got our first snowstorm. It was the most snow I had ever seen fall in one night. The kids were out of school, and I had to supervise the night shift, so Doug took me and picked me up. He was right. Even though he was experienced driving in the snow, he had to back up and gain some speed to get up the hill.

The kids had the most fun! They loved sledding downhill on the driveway and playing in the snow. Brad and Ciara played in the snow with them. Brad built a snow bear instead of a snowman. To me it looked just like the cola bear with a red hat and scarf.

I worked mostly as the night supervisor, so there was little time that I got to see the kids. Doug would take me and pick me up, so I didn't have to drive in the snow. I spent my morning having coffee and chatting with Rachelle if Brad was working.

It seemed like the snow was never going to go away, although it was pretty here in the mountains. The kids would sled down to the bus stop and use the sled to pull their things up in the afternoon. What a smart idea!

Brian called me to the office one day at work. I was incredibly nervous. What could I have done? There was nothing that I could think of. When I came into the office, he asked me to have a seat. Then he complimented me on my work that I had been doing at the pharmacy and asked me how I felt about being promoted to assistant store manager. I was not expecting that.

About that time the district manager came into the office, and Brian introduced me to Mr. Fisher. He told me that Mr. Fisher would be going over all the details with me and walked out, leaving me in the office.

Mr. Fisher said that he had heard nothing but good things about me and felt with my experience that I would be a great fit for the position. Once he told me all the benefits that came along with it as well as the salary, there was no turning it down.

The only downfall was I would have to take a pharmacy technician course and become certified. That was six weeks long and, in another town, starting in two weeks. After that, I would have to train for four weeks in a store in Vermont. I accepted the offer and would figure out the transportation issues later. I thanked him for this wonderful opportunity.

When Doug picked me up, I was so excited to tell him about it. He angrily asked me how I planned to get back and forth. I told him that I figured it was a wonderful opportunity for me and a lot more money for us that we could come up with a plan.

That night when we got home, I took a shower and got ready for bed. I prayed and thanked God for everything he did for my family every day and if this was the opportunity for me to help supply the transportation I needed.

The next morning Doug told me that his mom would take him to work when she went in, after all they worked together. Then he could take her Jeep home and pick her up when she got off. He would take me the first couple of days to make sure I knew where I was going.

Finally, after six weeks of driving back and forth and taking the class, it was the day of the test. I was having test anxiety again. I felt that I would do well, but I was extremely nervous. I did not want to disappoint Brian.

I would not have the results back for a couple of days. However, I thought I passed. I was going to stop by the store to let Brian know.

When I got to the pharmacy and told him I had completed the class, he said, "That's great! Now you will have to go to a Vermont store and shadow a store manager for four weeks. Go home and rest up. As soon as I hear something, I will let you know."

I replied, "Sounds good. I will talk to you soon."

A couple of days went by, and Brian finally called. He said I had done well on my test and was now a certified pharmacy technician. He gave me the store number, manager's name, and address of the store in Vermont where I would train for four weeks. Training would start on Monday. It was only Thursday, so I had a few days to figure out the ride situation. Doug was home, so I told him the good news. He called his mom and told her.

The next day, Doug and I would take a drive while the kids were in school and map it out for me. His sister said I could use her car, that she was going to sell it since she just bought a van.

When the kids came home from school, I told them about the test I passed and that I would start training on Monday for the full four weeks.

I let them play outside for thirty minutes while I got dinner started, and then they would do their homework. Since we had moved up here, I noticed they did better if they had a break from school before doing homework. They loved playing outside too, and if I made them do homework first, it became too dark to go outside after. Mama called and let me know that Anna had a baby boy on January 6, Daddy's birthday. How special was that? I know Daddy would have been so happy to share his birthday with his grandson.

They went sledding down the driveway and had made a fort out of pallets about halfway down the driveway on a cleared piece of land. We had a bullhorn I'd shout in for them to come in. Since it was winter, we didn't have to worry about the mama bear and cubs.

I called them inside to do their homework while I finished cooking.

They always came when called. They knew that I would ground them from outdoors. They came in and did homework. After dinner, they had to take baths. Then we watched a little TV, and I put them to bed with prayers, hugs, and kisses.

The next morning after the kids got on the bus, Doug and I went for a drive into Vermont to make sure I knew where I was going. I'm glad we did too because I had to go up on a mountain covered in snow. Going down would be the scary part. The road had a lot of curves in it. I hated driving in snow even on flat roads. We went back down, and he showed me how to maneuver the car on the curvy hill. It was about an hour drive one way.

Doug and I went to get the car from his sisters. The kids stayed and hung out in the yard with Brad while we were gone. He was like a big kid himself, loved playing in the snow with the kids.

The car was a stick shift, and I hadn't driven one in an awfully long time. So I was glad that I was getting the practice. We stopped and filled up the gas tank. I hoped that I could handle the stick going up and down the mountain.

The next morning Doug warmed and deiced the car for me. I got down on my knees and prayed for God to forgive me for my sins and to please protect me on my drive both ways.

I got in the car and headed out. I was so nervous. I left extra early to make sure to get there on time. The roads seemed worse today. I didn't turn on the radio, drove extra slowly, and prayed to God the whole drive there.

I made it. Thank you, Jesus! I sat in the car until I stopped shaking as I still had to walk across the icy parking lot to get inside the pharmacy.

The day went by quickly. Everything she was showing me I was already doing at the main store. The manager let me go a little early since it would be my first drive down the mountain. I did it like Doug taught me along with prayer. I almost made it home before dark. Now to get the car up the driveway. After three failed attempts, I blinked my lights and honked the horn for Doug to get it up the hill.

He had been watching me out the window, laughing at me. It upset me that he just laughed and didn't offer to help.

I felt better when I got inside and was greeted by the kids with hugs and smelled dinner cooking. The kids already had baths and homework done. We ate dinner and watched a couple of TV shows. Then I tucked them in and said prayers. David wanted to say them. It was sweet that he prayed for God to get me safely to and from work tomorrow. Then I took a shower and got ready for bed too.

I woke up to find we had even more snow on the ground. While I finished getting dressed, Doug deiced and warmed the car again for me. I left even earlier and was glad because the roads were so much more dangerous than yesterday. I had another conversation with God all the way there, thanking him so much as I pulled into the parking lot again.

Once again, I showed the manager that I already knew what she was to train me on this day. We sat in the office and went over the training packet. She had me show her what I hadn't been trained on yet. After I highlighted those sections, she said we could cover this in less than a week. That meant I only had to drive up here a few more days instead of weeks. I couldn't wait to tell Brian, Doug, and the kids.

It was time to go home. On the way down the mountain a tire blew out and I almost lost control. I shouted for Jesus to take the wheel, and I made it safely to the bottom of the mountain. Luckily, I had a prepaid cell phone for emergencies with me. I called Doug, and he got to me as quickly as he could. I was so happy to see him. He changed the tire and followed me home.

Rachelle was watching Lana and David, so I went to get them. Brad had made calzones for dinner, and the kids had already eaten. She offered me some, so I accepted and shared my day. I sent Lana upstairs to give Doug some calzone and tell him I would be up in a few minutes and for her to take a shower.

The next few days went by quickly and safely. I had completed my training. Now I would be working more hours but making better money with better benefits.

My shifts were either eight o'clock to six o'clock in the evening or eleven-thirty to nine-thirty in the evening. I didn't like the evening shift because I didn't get to eat dinner with the kids or tuck them in. Brian made my title official by putting my name and title on the sign in the entryway under his name and title.

CHAPTER FIFTY-THREE

It was spring of 2005, and Marie's daughter, Nicole, was graduating high school. I had my ticket and was flying home. I told the kids that I was going out of town for work. I was going to surprise them with Lacy coming back with me. While the kids were in school, Doug took me to the airport. I rented a car and drove to Marie's. It was so good to see and hug her. We visited for a while. Then I went to pick up Lacy. She would be going to the graduation with me. We also squeezed in a visit with Mamaw and Elsa while I was in town.

When we got to New York, Doug picked us up at the airport. We were going to his mom's house where many relatives were waiting to meet Lacy. Lana and David had no idea what was going on. They only knew that I was coming home. We dropped Lacy off right up the road from Jan's and told her to walk up in the yard.

When Doug and I got out of the car, Lana and David greeted me. We walked up to the front porch where everyone was seated for a cookout. Lacy walked up in the yard. I heard someone ask, "Who's that?" About that time, David took off running, shouting, "Lacy!" He squeezed her tightly while tears ran down his cheeks. He was so happy to see his sister. It took Lana a little bit to realize what was going on, and then she happily greeted her sister.

I had told Lacy that I would not beg her to move to New York with us. She was here to visit for two weeks. I did kind of hint around a few times by saying, "You could just stay here." Lana and David asked her a couple of times. One day she came up to me and said she wanted to move here but was afraid her dad would be mad at her.

About two days before she was to fly home, she called her dad and let him know that she wanted to stay here. I think he was shocked that she had changed her mind, but he was not mad at her.

I had been having some health issues and went to see an OBGYN someone referred me to. Dr. Wiggins was very patient, kind, and caring. She examined me and took some tests.

A couple of days later, Dr. Wiggins called and asked me to come in to see her. I did not like her tone. Was it bad news? Usually, when the doctor asked you to come in for results, it was not good. She had an opening the next afternoon.

Sleep did not come easy on this night. I lay in bed mostly thinking the worst and praying for God to let the results be something curable or that could be managed.

The next afternoon could not come fast enough. Then there was the waiting once we arrived to be called back to the office. I anxiously waited for the results.

Finally, my name was called, and I followed the nurse to an exam room. She told me that the doctor would be right with me. Soon after Dr. Wiggins came into the room and sat down on the stool in front of me. She said, "Daisy, I am afraid I have some bad news to share with you." I told her that I knew it was not good or she would have told me on the phone.

She said that she asked me here today so we could talk about some options." Then she told me the results showed I had cancerous polyps in my uterus and cancer cells on my cervix. When I heard the word *cancer*, that was all I heard. She suggested we schedule a hysterectomy at once. She had the nurse set up the appointment for surgery the following week. I would have to stay at least one, maybe two nights.

I left the doctor's office in a daze. This news was shocking. Doug told me that she had said she was confident that all of it would be removed with surgery.

Doug took me by the pharmacy so I could get the necessary paperwork for a leave of absence. Dr. Wiggins said I would need at least six weeks off.

Doug's stepmom, Deena, was planning to come to the house the night before the surgery so she could cook and stay with the kids while I was in the hospital.

We arrived at the hospital at the scheduled time. I was called back to a room where I would also stay after the surgery. I had some time before the surgery would start, so I prayed.

"Father, please forgive me of my sins. Be with and guide the doctor's hands to remove all the cancer cells from my body. Watch over the kids for me and keep them safe while we are away. Reassure them that their mom will be fine. Lord, please help me to have a speedy recovery as well. Thank you for sending Deena to take care of the kids. I ask this be your will. In Jesus's name, amen."

Once the surgery was over, I woke up in the recovery room in severe pain. A nurse came over and gave me a shot of morphine. Once that kicked in, I felt much better. A few moments later, I was taken back to the hospital room where Doug was waiting.

The nurse said I should rest today and tomorrow they would get me up to walk around. After I was able to go to the restroom, I would get to go home. This was when I noticed Doug's attitude change. I had never seen or heard him be mean before. He was always so laid-back, never raised his hand or voice.

He said to me, "You need to get up as early as you can and walk, use the restroom, and get out of here. One night is enough."

When a nurse was in the room, he was nice but not when we were alone. It made me feel alone. He asked me to see if they could get me up walking today. I told him that I had just come from having a major surgery and he was going to have to be a little more patient.

I said, "If you want to, just go home. There is no need for you to be here." He stood up and said he would be back in the morning.

It was at this time that I feared going home with him tomorrow or the next day. Thankfully, Rachelle lived next door to us. If I felt that I was in danger, I could just call her.

I prayed for the kids to be safe while I was away and for the doctor to have succeeded with removing everything from my body so I might have a speedy recovery. I also thanked him for Deena being at the house to take care of the kids and that I would be able to walk and go to the bathroom so that I might go home with them. I thanked the Lord for everything he had done for me and my family.

Doug arrived early the next morning. He was rude to me as he woke me up, saying, "Come on, let's get you up to start walking."

I was at least wanting to wait for the nurse to tell me that. I hadn't even had breakfast yet. I said to him, "I will wait until after breakfast to walk."

He said angrily, "Well then, I will be back later." Then he left.

I went back to sleep until they brought in breakfast. The nurse asked me if I wanted to try to sit up in the chair to eat. With her aid, I got out of bed and into the chair. I finished eating, and she asked if I was ready to walk. I was up walking when Doug came back.

He said, "Good, you are up and about. Looks like you will be going home today."

I told him to slow down, that I hadn't even been to the bathroom yet.

I walked back to the room and was going to lie down when he pulled on my arm and told me to go to the bathroom. I went to the bathroom and sat down on the toilet. When he walked out, I asked the Lord what I had gotten myself into. I could tell I was not going to have help at home.

I was able to go to the restroom, so Doug asked the nurse if I could go home now. She told him that she would let the doctor know and get back to us as soon as she heard anything.

As a couple of hours went by, all Doug did was complain. When the nurse came back in, she asked me to go to the bathroom again. After I finished, she said that she would get the discharge paperwork going.

"Finally," Doug said. A few minutes later, she came back with a wheelchair, some prescriptions, and paperwork for me. Doug went to bring the car around.

I had to go to the pharmacy to get my prescriptions since one was a narcotic. Since I worked here, and the pharmacist knew that I was in pain, she got them filled rather quickly. Once we arrived home, I went to bed. Deena brought in some crackers, ginger ale, and medicine for me. I took them and dozed off. I slept until the kids came home from school. They came in to give me hugs and tell me that they were glad I was home and okay.

Doug brought my dinner to the bedroom on a tray. He also brought in my medicine. After I ate and took the medicine, I went back to sleep. It wasn't long that I woke up to go to the bathroom. I went back to bed in a great deal of pain. I just thought I needed to give the medicine time to kick in.

When Doug came to bed, I got up to go to the bathroom. I was still hurting, but it was worse now. I went back and forth from the bed to the bathroom. Finally, I just lay on the bathroom floor. A little while later, I yelled for Doug. I told him to take me to the hospital, that I was in severe pain and the pills weren't helping. He angrily got dressed to take me.

"Maybe I came home too soon," I told him.

The nurses took me right back to an exam room when I got there. The doctor said he believed it was bladder retention. I told him that I had been several times and didn't think that was it. He did an ultrasound on my bladder and said it was full. He had a nurse catharize me, and I received instant relief. They sent me home with a catheter and told me to follow up with my doctor in two days.

I called Dr. Wiggins's office and spoke to her nurse about the bladder issue. She told me that I had to clamp the catheter off every two hours for thirty minutes. After two days of that, I had to do it for an hour. I would have to do that until I saw Dr. Wiggins the next week.

After the week, I had an appointment to see her. That morning after I woke up, I had to clamp it off until I got to her office. They took the catheter out and told me to go to the restroom. I was able to go on my own. Thank you, Lord. I had prayed the night before and the morning of my appointment for me to be able to go on my own and that all the cancer was gone.

Dr. Wiggins came in and told me that she would see me in five weeks for my checkup and made sure she got everything, that it was too soon to tell right now.

I still had cramps and pain from the surgery but was so glad to be rid of the catheter. We went home, and I waited for the kids to get home. Maybe they would play a game with me to pass the time.

CHAPTER FIFTY-FOUR

Finally, after five weeks I was ready for my appointment. The kids and I had prayed many nights for this day. Hopefully all the cancer was removed successfully.

I waited in the waiting room for the nurse to call me back. It was so quiet in there. All you could hear was the ticking of the clock. While I sat there, I prayed for God to please let there be good news today and the cancer was gone. I had faith in him that it was gone from my body.

The nurse called my name as she held the door open. I walked back with her to the exam room. She took my vitals and told me to get undressed then Dr. Wiggins would be in to examine me.

I lay down on the table after I got undressed, and Dr. Wiggins knocked on the door. I nervously told her to come on in. She took a sample to send into the lab. I would have to wait for the results. She said it would only be a day or two, and she would call me once she received them.

Two days went by, and Dr. Wiggins called. She said, "I have good news. It looks like we removed all the cancer cells. You are in the clear. You will need to come back in six months for a follow-up test."

I cried tears of joy. The cancer was gone. "Thank you, God, for guiding Dr. Wiggins's hands to successfully remove all the diseased cells from my body. Please allow me to remain cancer-free. In Jesus's name, amen."

Doug was at work, so I went down to share the news with Rachelle. I had to tell someone. I was so happy. She hugged me tightly and cried happy tears with me. Then I heard the kids coming up the driveway. I went out to meet them at the door and tell them the good news too.

It wasn't long before Doug made it home, and I told him, "Dr. Wiggins called me today with good news."

He just smiled and said, "That's great." Then he went and got on the computer. He started spending hours and hours at a time on the computer. He wasn't cooking anymore or hardly even talking to me. He just told me that he and a man in England were starting up a company.

I got a call from the Arkansas County District Attorney. Apparently, Jimmy turned himself in. He called 911 and told the dispatcher that he had molested my girls and was thinking of doing it to his own children. She said that if it went to trial, the kids would have to come into town and testify against him.

When I went grocery shopping, I made sure to get things that the kids could make for themselves while I was at work. I would start back on Monday.

As I tucked them in that night, I told them I needed them to be responsible and do their homework and take their baths while I worked. I had a feeling that Doug was not going to be much help. I took a shower, picked out my clothes for work, and went to bed too. Doug was still on the computer.

The alarm went off that morning. I told the kids to get up and get ready for school while I got ready for work. I drove them to the bus stop and went to work. Everyone was as happy to see me back as I was to be back.

The day went by quickly, and it was time to go home. I would cook since I worked the earlier shift today. I knew Doug would be glued to the computer. Ciara was in Lana's room when I got home playing with her Bratz dolls. Lana said she had done her homework, so I let them play while I cooked. David was in his room playing a video game but told me that he had done his homework too.

We had recently bought a male and female chihuahua, thinking of breeding them when they were old enough. They were flown in from a breeder in Alabama. We named them Bam Bam and Pebbles.

I made a quick dinner and asked Doug if he was going to eat. He said he'd get a plate later. Lana asked if Ciara could stay and eat with us. I had her give Rachelle a call to make sure it was okay. The five of us sat down at the table. David said grace, and we talked about our day as we ate our dinner.

After we ate, I had Lana walk Ciara home. Then we watched a couple of TV shows and got ready for bed so we could do it all again the next day. We went into David's room to say our prayers. I told them that I trusted Lacy to make sure that the kids got their homework done tomorrow because I had to work the evening shift. She would make sure that they heated their TV dinners up right too.

When I came home from work the next evening, the kids were in the bed. Doug, of course, was on the computer. I fixed me something to eat, took a shower, and went to bed.

We never even talked anymore. At least we didn't fight. I guess that was a good thing. Rachelle had said that Ciara had asked her why I was always working and he was at home on the computer. If he did go to work, it was only for a couple of hours, and he was in a hurry to get home on the computer. I always went to bed before him and never heard him come to bed.

The Arkansas County District Attorney called me to say court was the following week, and they had bought airline tickets for us all to come into town to testify.

Doug took us to the airport, and Beth picked us up. The next morning when we were getting ready, the district attorney called and told me that Jimmy had accepted a plea bargain and the girls did not have to go to court. Jimmy was sentenced to twenty years for rape. She told us to enjoy our trip home. We spent four nights here. I used Leena's car and went to visit Jolie and Marie the day before we left. Beth took us back to the airport on our departure day, and Doug picked us up.

CHAPTER FIFTY-FIVE

October 2007, I came home from work one evening and we all ate dinner. The kids had finished their homework, and we watched some TV. The kids had baths, we said our prayers, and I gave them a kiss good night.

Doug and I were watching a movie. The dogs were over a year old, and Pebbles was in heat. I mentioned maybe that she could get pregnant. He was finishing a big bowl of ice cream and hatefully said, "She might."

I said, "You don't have to be mean about it. I see them at least trying soon, anyways."

The next thing I remember was him standing up and the ceramic bowl coming toward my head. Then I woke up in a big puddle of blood on the floor. Lacy came in the living room and saw me. Doug came in with a towel and tried to touch my head. I told him to get away from me. Lana came in, and I told her to call 911. She was too nerve wrecked to call, so Lacy did. Doug went downstairs on the cell phone. David got up terribly upset and was going to hit Doug with a plate. I told him to stop and stay away from him.

Lacy called 911/ I told her to call Rachelle, who had just recently moved a few miles away. She informed Rachelle that she needed to come over as soon as possible. Doug had hurt me, badly. I sat on the stairs and scooted down to the entryway. As I made it outside, the neighbor came out. When she saw me, she ran in her house and grabbed another towel. The one I had been holding on my head was completely saturated in blood. I was trying my hardest to remain conscious, but as soon as I saw Rachelle had arrived, I blacked out.

When I regained consciousness, I was in the ambulance. As they took me from the ambulance to the ER, I saw Rachelle. They sent me back for a head CT. I lost consciousness again. When I woke up, the doctor was flushing ceramic out of my head, and Rachelle was holding my hand crying. The doctor told us that I had a fractured skull and was leaking cerebrospinal fluid from my nose. I was incredibly lucky to be alive. I thanked God for that. They were going to try to treat it with IV caffeine infusions as well as saline infusions. I could not stay conscious.

I woke up, and Rachelle was sitting in a chair by my bed. She said "Good morning, sunshine" with a smile. She told me that I had been out for two days.

"The kids, where are my kids?" I asked hoarsely.

She said that they were staying with the church minister and family. She let me know that the dogs were with them as well. That made me feel good knowing that they were being taken care of. Rachelle went to let the nurse know that I was awake.

She came in right away and took my vitals. She sat my bed up, and once I was completely in a sitting position, I lost consciousness. She laid me back down right away. I wasn't out long and asked her what happened. She said there was still too much pressure being applied to my injury when sitting straight up. I would have to stay laid down until my brain injury healed more.

A police officer came in to get my statement. I asked if Doug was in jail, and he told me that he was out on bail at this time. We completed the paperwork for a restraining order. We had just bought a new car that was in my name. I asked Rachelle if she would go get it for me and take it to her property. An officer went with her so there would be no problems.

I remained in the hospital on bed rest for almost three weeks total before being released. They had to make sure there was no more leakage and that I could sit up without blacking out. I stayed in touch with Mama and kept her up to date on my condition.

The day I was released, Rachelle took me to get the kids. The minster's wife thought it would be best if I stayed with them a couple of nights before going back home. I agreed to stay with them, and Rachelle went home. I called Mama to let her know that I was out of the hospital.

A victim's advocate reached out to me. She was going to help the kids and I get back to Texas. She said it would take at least two to three weeks to complete everything. She would try to make it happen before Thanksgiving. It was already November, and she didn't think that it could be finished in time.

I had to testify before the grand jury about what had happened. They had my blood-soaked work shirt and towels along with some pictures as evidence. They had agreed to take it to trial and were going to charge Doug with attempted murder. When it went to trial, I might have to come back to testify, but the state would pay for the trip and accommodations.

Rachelle and Brad brought my car to me. The kids and I went back to the house so we could start packing. I really didn't like being back here. Neither did the kids. David asked if he could sleep with me. I liked that idea too since I didn't want to be alone.

Before we went to sleep, the girls came into my room, and I prayed, "Dear Heavenly Father, thank you so much for giving the kids a safe place to stay while I was in the hospital. Thank you for taking care of me and putting me on the road to recovery. We ask for you to please make it possible for us to go back home to Texas with our family soon. Until we can do that, please continue to keep us safe. I ask that this be your will. In Jesus's name, amen."

The church bought Lana and David airline tickets to fly back to Texas for Thanksgiving. Beth was going to pick them up and let them stay with her until we got back. She was happy to have them for Thanksgiving.

Their last night home, Darren wanted to stay and go with me to the airport. He and his mom were just sick about what his dad had done to me. Darren was a sweet boy. I would miss those kids. Darren's mom told me that Doug had pushed her through a wall when she was pregnant with DJ. This violence was not new. She said she would testify if needed.

We had to get up at four o'clock in the morning to get Lana and David to the airport. It was snowing, and I got lost. However, we did manage to get them there on time. I dropped Darren off at his mom's house on the way home. The snow was really coming down, but Lacy and I finally made it back.

The victim's advocate was going to pay for a U-Haul truck, trailer, gas, hotel, food, and fly someone up to drive the truck to Texas for us. I called Luke and asked him if he could do it. We could leave the day after Thanksgiving. Alyssa told him to do it. She wanted us home safely. Memaw was going to let us stay with her. She had been lonely since Pepaw passed away.

I called Eugene at his parents' house and told him what had happened and asked him if he could help us unload the U-Haul once we made it back. He said yes. He told me to call his cell phone and keep him posted on how far we made it each day.

Wednesday, the boys from the youth group and the minister packed up the U-Haul for us. We would be ready to go as soon as Luke made it here.

Lacy and I had Thanksgiving with the minister's family. They had been so good to us through this whole ordeal. I knew that God was taking care of us and everything was working out.

Friday afternoon, I picked Luke up from the airport. We stayed at a hotel in town since everything was packed up in the truck. All we had to do was put the car on the trailer and we were ready to go. I took Luke by to meet Brad and Rachelle. Also, I wanted to tell them goodbye. Over the years of living up here, Rachelle had become my best friend, and Brad had never really cared for Doug.

Lacy and I said our goodbyes to Brad and Rachelle. We went to the hotel to get a good night's rest before the drive home started tomorrow. I called Eugene to let him know that we were leaving in the morning.

We got up early to go to the house, put the car on the trailer, and get started on our long drive back to Texas. We went about halfway then got a room for the night and ordered a pizza. My head was pounding. I knew it was from the injury and sitting up for the duration of the trip so far. Tomorrow I would take a pain pill before we left.

I prayed and gave thanks to God for keeping us safe on our journey so far and to just surround us with a shield of protection until we safely made it back to Texas. Then I called Eugene to let him know we were in Ohio, which was about halfway home. While I called him, Lacy took the dogs out for a little walk.

I took a shower, ate some pizza, took some medicine, said my prayers, and went to sleep. Luke wanted to get an early start the next morning and drive all the way back to Texas.

We woke up at five o'clock in the morning, got dressed, grabbed a couple of muffins from the continental breakfast, and we walked the dogs for a minute before we were on the road. I made sure to take some medicine as we started out.

Stopping a couple of times on the road to get gas, food, let the dogs out, or go to the bathroom was about all we did. Other than that, we kept moving.

It was nice to get back to familiar surroundings. We finally made it to Memaw's house. She met us outside. Luke had already called Alyssa to come and pick him up. Lacy walked the dogs and let them stretch their legs while he was going to take my car off the trailer, but it wouldn't start.

When Alyssa arrived, he directed her to park next to the car and jumped the battery off. Once it started, he took it off the trailer. I thanked him for getting us home safely. He told everyone goodbye, got in his car with Alyssa, and they went home.

I called Mama and told her we were back safely on Texas soil at Memaw's. Then I called Beth to let her know we had made it and that I would be over tomorrow to pick up Lana and David. Memaw had dinner on the table for us. It was nice to be eating southern cooking again. After dinner, Lacy and I took care of the dishes. I walked the dogs, called Eugene, took a shower, said prayers, and went to bed after I thanked Memaw for letting us stay with her.

I woke up early so I could go pick up the kids. I was ready to see them and for us to all be together again. When we got back to Memaw's, I called Eugene and Autumn. She had told me that she would help unload the U-Haul too.

Memaw had a big empty room in the barn and said we could store my stuff in there. Eugene drove the U-Haul into the pasture and backed up to the barn. The four of us, counting Lacy, got it unloaded quickly. Eugene did most of the heavy lifting.

Dinner was ready, and Memaw asked Autumn and Eugene if they wanted to stay and eat. Autumn said she needed to go home, but he stayed and ate with us.

Lana and David played with the dogs for a while. I was going to enroll them back into school tomorrow. I gave them baths, and we said our prayers. We thanked God for helping us get back safely and allowing us to all be together again. Lana slept in the room with Lacy, and David slept with me. I called Eugene and thanked him for helping us. He told me to call him tomorrow and he would drive the U-Haul so I could turn it in.

CHAPTER FIFTY-SIX

I woke up and took the kids to the school to enroll them. When we finished that, I called Eugene. He came over and I followed him to the U-Haul return. Then I drove him back to Memaw's. She asked him to stay for dinner again. She told me that she really liked him.

The kids started back to school the next day. My car payment was about to be due. I had no clue how I was going to pay it. I started looking for a job in the small town we lived in, but no one was hiring.

I called Mr. and Mrs. Powers' office to see if they were hiring. When I told them I now had office managing experience, they said they needed an office manager in the primary office. I was to meet Mr. Powers there the next afternoon.

Eugene had offered to pay my car payment for me. I agreed only if he would let me pay him back. We were talking on the phone a lot, or he would come over for dinner. Dean had come over to see the kids too. He wanted them to stay with him next weekend. That was fine with me.

Eugene asked me to come over and watch a movie with him. We went to Blockbuster and saw Dean and the kids there getting movies also.

When the movie was over, Eugene walked me to my car. It was then we mutually kissed. I didn't see that coming, but it felt right. I asked him to the Sadie Hawkins dance in high school, and in 2000 he had asked me out. This time it was mutual.

I wanted to go spend some time with Marie. It just so happened that she was having a garage sale and wanted my help. I had Eugene take my dryer out there to sell. I also took some things Doug had bought me that I wanted to get rid of. I wanted Marie to meet Eugene too. I stayed three nights with her. The garage sale did quite well. I sold everything I brought.

I went to work for the Powers in the primary office for a few months. I came home every day with a migraine. I think I was trying too fast to get back to work. However, I had bills to pay. One afternoon Eugene called and told me Pebbles was having her puppies. Mr. Powers told me I could go home. By the time I made it home, she had the third and last puppy. Bam Bam did not know what to think. Good thing Eugene was there because he had to help Pebbles out. I guess you could say we were dating. I felt from God that it was the right time for us to be together after knowing each other for so many years. We never missed a day seeing each other, and he was so good to me. David did not really like the idea. I was not looking for a relationship, it was too soon, but it just kind of found me.

I went to the local bank and applied to refinance my car. I only owed $1,500 so I did not see it being an issue. I got a nice-sized loan on it, so I could slow down for a little while. I quit my job and looked for a place to live so we could move out of Memaw's. David was going to move in with Dean for a while.

I found a cute little three-bedroom two-bath house a few blocks from Eugene's parents. When his mother, Trisha, found out we were a couple, she let me know that she was incredibly happy about it by saying, "I knew it was only a matter of time. You know what they say, mother always knows." I didn't have a bed since I had given Memaw mine. Eugene had a futon in his room, so he let me use his bed.

The house next door was throwing out a playpen. I had Lacy go get it so that we could keep the puppies in it. Lana asked if we could name the puppies. I thought she was getting too attached to them. Every day after school she took them outside to run around. She called the two bigger ones Potato and Tomato. Memaw was going to get the runt, which we named Precious. We sold Potato and Tomato when they were six weeks old and gave Precious to Memaw.

Richard called me one afternoon. I wasn't going to answer but thought something might be wrong with Mama. He was calling to say he might know of a job for me. He gave me a name and phone number to call. Her name was Joette. She was starting up a weight loss center and looking for consultants to train and hire.

I gave Joette a call right away. She wanted to meet me at a coffee shop the next afternoon. As it turned out, my daddy used to give her mother rides to work when she worked at the depot where the fire station was. I felt I had a nice interview with her.

Not long after I left the coffee shop, she called me to tell me I had the job. She wanted me to meet her at a nice steak house in town that evening. She was introducing the staff and updating us to when we would begin training.

We began training the following week in a conference room at a hotel in town. Training was a two-week course followed by a certification exam. Construction was still in progress at the center.

There was a ribbon-cutting ceremony upon opening the center. I continued to work for her part-time at the center for a few months. Then Eugene was offered a job transfer to a more central Texas town. I hated to give my notice; I really liked the job. However, I knew there would be excellent job opportunities where we were going.

The kids were out of school for the summer when we moved. Eugene went down to the city to look for a place to live. I prayed as he was gone that God would help to find and place us in a safe location.

Eugene came back and had found us a nice three-bedroom two-bath townhome. It only had one downfall, and we could only keep one dog. I gave Pebbles to a girl I was working with, and we kept Bam Bam. I found a job at a weight loss center a few miles from the townhouse. I worked there for a couple of months and was promoted to sales manager. I ranked number one in sales out of a total of twenty-one centers six months in a row.

I had just made it to work one day when Anna called me to tell me that Wes had passed away. He had overdosed on his medicine. Even though I had not seen or talked to him, it still hurt me to hear this news.

CHAPTER FIFTY-SEVEN

Lacy was planning to move out right before her eighteenth birthday. She had been working after school and weekends at a fast-food restaurant a couple of miles from the townhouse and had saved up enough money for a down payment on a car. I had told her that if she was moving out that she was going to have to pay her own car insurance. I was working with the insurance company to get her own account. Since it was so late to get everything faxed to them, they said it would be Monday morning before we could finish it up.

Instead of waiting for Monday, Lacy didn't come back home. She was impatient and just took off. I was so upset. I was so scared she would get into an accident on the long drive and not have any insurance. I cried and prayed and cried and prayed for hours. She would not answer her cell phone, so I didn't know if she made it or not. I just had to trust my faith in God to get her there safely. I gave it to the Lord.

Lana managed to get in touch with her the next day and told her how badly it had hurt me for her to leave that way. All she had to do was be patient and wait until Monday. Sometimes I felt Lana was the big sister. She was very mature for her age. All the kids were teenagers now. How could this be? Time was going by too quickly. Only Lana was living with Eugene and me. The two of them were becoming close. Lana was very artistic, and Eugene would help her with projects she would do.

The night before Valentine's Day at midnight, Eugene asked me to marry him. He was so nervous and excited. Of course I said yes. I found out later that he was sweet to ask Lana how she felt about him asking me to marry him. She told him it was okay. I had to work the next day, so I got to show off my ring to all my coworkers.

Eugene's parents were in town staying with his brother, Rory. His wife, Kara, had recently had a baby girl. They named her Avery. We went over there to visit with everyone. As I passed Avery to Kara, Eugene's mom caught a glimpse of the ring. She asked, "Did I see what I think I saw on your hand? Hold it up." I happily held out my hand to show the ring. She said, "Oh my gosh! When did this happen?"

I replied, "Just last night." Then everyone asked to see it and wanted to know when the wedding was. We told them we hadn't had a chance to talk about that yet.

It wasn't long after this that we moved into a nice house in the same town. Only no dogs were allowed in the house. We made a doghouse for Bam Bam in the fenced-in backyard.

One morning after Eugene left for work, his mom called me crying. She asked if he was home, and I told her she just missed him. She then told me that his best friend, Jerry, had been killed on his motorcycle. I had also known Jerry since I was three from church. I began crying too. Then Eugene walked in the door because he had forgotten his wallet. I told his mom I would call her back, and I broke the news to Eugene. He called his job and let them know what happened. I also called my job, and we drove back to our hometown after Lana got home from school.

We stayed in town until after Jerry's funeral. It was hard for me because he was buried in the same cemetery as my daddy, which brought back a lot of memories. We went back home after the funeral.

I was sitting in the backyard playing with Bam Bam one day on my day off, a Wednesday, a few weeks later when Nichole, Marie's daughter, called my phone. I answered, "Hey, girl! How are you doing?" She asked me if I was sitting down. "Nichole, what's wrong?" I asked.

She said, "Mama is gone." I asked what she meant. She then told me, "Mama died Monday, Daisy. She's gone."

I fell to my knees screaming, "No! It can't be."

She told me that they were having her cremated, and her memorial was the next day. I couldn't get off from work since it wasn't a family member without more notice. I asked Nichole why she didn't tell me sooner so I could have asked off. They had been living in Louisiana with Marie's mom since she was ill. So there was no way to make the trip in only one day.

CHAPTER FIFTY-EIGHT

I had applied for a promotion for center manager. It would be a longer drive, but so much more money and so much more experience for me. I was so nervous for my phone interview with corporate directors. It would be a few weeks before I would know if I'd gotten the position.

A couple of weeks later, I received a phone call that my Mamaw was in the hospital. Eugene and I arranged a couple of days off so we could go and see her. I prayed for God to heal her and keep her safe.

The day we came back home, while I was at work, I got a call that she had a stroke. I called Eugene and had him meet me at home so we could go back to our hometown.

It was June, so Lana was out of school. I stayed with Mamaw for a week, using my vacation time. She never knew what my brother, J.R., had done to me and was asking me where he was. I put my anger for him aside and called J.R.'s now ex-wife, Cindy. I asked her if she knew how I could get in touch with him and told her about Mamaw. She gave me his number, and I gave it to Joe so he could call him.

The next day he arrived at the hospital, and so did Anna. Mamaw was so happy to see the three of us together. She just smiled so big with bright eyes. I would do anything for my Mamaw. Even if it meant I had to stand next to J.R.

He hadn't seen her in fifteen years and was just talking to everyone like no time had passed. It was unbelievable to me. I stayed at the hospital for a week with Mamaw. I sponged her mouth when it was dry, brushed her hair, washed her face, talked to her, and gave her many kisses.

They had Mamaw moved to a nursing home, and a family member stayed with her every night. We went back home and had planned to come back on the Fourth of July. That morning the phone rang at six o'clock. I knew she was gone. She had passed away in her sleep peacefully.

Why had there been so much loss these past few months? Why had God taken so much from us in such a brief time? Had I disappointed him and gotten off path? I felt so broken inside. Was I being punished? I should have been there more for Marie and Mamaw. Marie had been in pain for so long. I had prayed for God to end her pain. Was that what he had done, just not in the way I wanted? I had so many questions for God.

On the way to Mamaw's funeral, I got a call from work. I got the promotion I applied for. It was as if I was on a roller-coaster ride of emotions. I was happy I had gotten the promotion one minute then sad about Mamaw the next.

When her funeral was over, we were going to go back home. Lana was going to stay a week or two so she could visit her cousins, Beth and Leena. David was staying the week with Leena too. He had gone with us to the funeral. He said that he wanted to move in with us when school started. It would be good to have him around again.

It was a lot longer drive to the center that I had started managing. I had Eugene take me and pick me up for a while. All the traffic made me nervous. I wasn't used to big city driving, and it was three towns over. It took us forty-five minutes at least to get home.

I managed that center for a few months, bringing its profits up 25 percent year over year. Then I was promoted to a newer center as manager. It was a little less of a drive and in a nicer part of town.

After a few months of working here, Eugene and I began to make wedding plans. We visited home before the wedding about every other weekend, getting things in order.

March 2010, the venue for the wedding was a nice little church in our hometown. Pink and brown were the colors of choice, with family pews marked with pink satin bows. My longtime friend Kaye was my maid of honor, and Eugene's sister, Denae, came into town as a bridesmaid. They were both wearing satin dresses of brown. Denae's daughters, Katie and Olivia, as flower girls in beautiful pink ruffled dresses. Her son, Aiden, as ring bearer in his cute little tuxedo. I had planned for Nichole to stand in for her mom as a bridesmaid, but she was sick. Kara, Rory's wife, did the honor of taking her place at the last minute for me, wearing a formal pink dress. Their daughter, Avery, another smaller flower girl that stole the show with her ruffled pink dress and basket of pink petals she threw down and picked back up. Rory was Eugene's best man, wearing a black tuxedo accessorized with pink bow tie. His other friends, Justin, Ryan, and Clyde, were groomsmen. Their tuxedos had bow ties and cummerbunds in pink. My gorgeous wedding dress drug the ground as I came down the aisle, full of roses beaded in pearls. My something borrowed being from Denae, her beautiful veil; new charm bracelet from Eugene; blue garter around my thigh with a penny in my shoe—my attire was complete.

Our white three-tiered wedding cake had white sugar-spun roses and topped with two silver connecting hearts. Brown tablecloths covered the tables with clear bowls filled with pink crystals and floating candles, surrounded by big, clear diamond-shaped crystals, which made beautiful centerpieces.

Eugene's mom, Trisha, busied herself in the kitchen, making sure the food was nice and hot and everything perfect for her son's wedding day.

Having Mama and all three of my children there made it perfect for me. It was this day Lacy and I spoke again, which made me happy. I had missed her very much. I thanked God for this beautiful wedding day.

Lacy drove Lana and David home before school started. She stayed and visited for just a minute and drove back home. Before they made it home, Bam Bam had escaped the backyard through a hole in the fence. We searched for him sadly with no luck in finding him.

We went home to visit when we could since it wasn't too far of a drive. We would stay with Eugene's grandma. She had recently discovered she had cancer. So we wanted to see her as much as possible.

CHAPTER FIFTY-NINE

In late spring of 2011, Joette had purchased another weight loss center and called to offer me a promotion if I would come back to work for her. The centers were ninety miles away from each other. She wanted me to be a district manager and go back and forth between the two centers. I told her that I didn't feel my car would be good for driving back and forth. She said that she would purchase a company car that I could use to go between centers and would get a raise.

I prayed for God to give me a sign as to what I should do. Eugene's grandma had been so good to us, and I felt God was telling me that we needed to be there for her, and the job offer from Joette was another sign.

I accepted the position but did not start until the kids were out of school for the summer. We would move back to our hometown again, but it would mean that we would get stay with Eugene's grandma, and he would take care of her while I worked. Lana stayed with us, and David moved back in with his dad.

Eugene took care of his grandma until the end of September 2011, when she passed away. She had told us before she passed away that we could stay there if we wanted to.

One of Joette's centers weren't doing well in the economy, so she chose to close it down. I worked from home some and drove to the center ninety miles away two days a week. After doing that for some time, Joette really didn't need a district manager anymore. I offered to step out of the position. We continued to stay in Eugene's grandma's house until Lana graduated in May of 2013.

After Lana's graduation, she moved in with Beth, and Eugene and I were going to try our luck starting over in South Texas. I reached out to my friend Rhonda to see if she could find us an apartment. I prayed to God that we would find a place in a safe location. Once Rhonda found an apartment for us, I sent her a money order, and she went to pay the deposit for us.

I had left a few things stored in the barn at Memaw's, but when we went to get them, the room was empty. I asked Memaw about it, and she said maybe the man she had working the land had thrown them out. I was terribly disappointed as some of the things belonged to my parents. We packed up a U-Haul and proceeded to South Texas. Once we arrived and got settled in, Mama called me to let me know that Memaw had passed away. I wanted to go back for her funeral, but we just couldn't afford to make such a long drive again so soon. It was a nine-hour drive. So I sent condolences and flowers.

I lucked out thanks to Joette's help and found a job at a weight loss center. I worked there part-time for a few months. Then she let me go because business was too slow.

I put my faith in the Lord's hands. I knew he would provide a way for us to be able to make it work here. I continued to look for a job.

I found one as an office manager renting condominiums on the beach. I started working there in January 2014. The manager's name was Sage. She was a great trainer, and I was picking up on my tasks very quickly. All the condominiums were privately owned, and it took a while, but I got to know most owners by name.

The drive to the condominiums was long, so right before our lease was up, we looked for an apartment closer. We found one about ten minutes away.

I really enjoyed this job. Sage and I made a wonderful team. She would give me reports or projects with a deadline, and I always managed to finish days before that deadline. This became my favorite job. I never woke up and dreaded going to work. I got to enjoy God's great artwork every day. Working with that relaxing view just steps away was so soothing.

I helped a regular guest, Lori, find a condominium to purchase. Summertime was so busy, and the condominiums stayed rented out. I had to do housekeeping inspections to make sure everything was up to standards for guests and owners prior to check-in. There were several regular guests that stayed here. I became close with the groundskeeper, Nancy, and one family in particular that stayed at least two or three times a year. They were the Daltons, a great, very respectful Christian family with six children.

You could always find them out on the beach or beside the pool reading the Bible. They were an inspiration to me. I loved every minute I had to visit with them. The mother and father, Maggie and Derick; four girls, Breanna, Lilly, Hope, and Millie. Then there were the boys, Nick and Conner. They always made sure to stop by my office to say hello to me, and I looked forward to our prayer time.

In the winter, the rentals would fill up with what we called "Winter Texans" or couples that lived in the northern states that came to the south for warmer weather.

David was shipped off to military basic training a week after he graduated from high school. In September 2014, he graduated from basic training. It was a joyous occasion seeing this. I was proud of him for pursuing a career from something I only dreamed of for myself. He was deployed to Dubai for sixth months and enjoyed getting to go places that he had never thought he would go.

CHAPTER SIXTY

Eugene worked with my boss's husband, Earl, for a while and became close with some owners they had remodeled for. One couple told him to invite his family down for a visit and they could stay in their condominium.

Eugene's mom and dad came down a few times and stayed with us. By this time, Rory and Kara had three children—one girl, Avery, and two boys, Bryan and Boyce. Denae, Olivia, Katie, and Aiden came as well, was nice to have access to a condominium. It was great to have the whole family here on vacation. Lana came once with Eugene's parents. We took turns and flew Lacy or Lana down when they could get off work and take a vacation.

In February 2016, Trisha was diagnosed with lung cancer. We would drive home when we could, or she and Eugene's dad, Dane, would come down while she was still able because she loved it here at the beach. We loved having them and always hated to see them leave.

Every day I prayed that Trisha be healed. I asked God to take the cancer away and for the treatments to work. She told me she wasn't going anywhere, that she wanted to see her grandchildren grow up. I called her when I could, and there were times that she did not want to talk.

In March Lacy called me to tell me that Dean was in the hospital, and they did not think that he would make it. He had pneumonia and was septic. He was in the hospital for a couple of weeks, and he passed away. Now I was the only parent my kids had.

Eugene and I went into town so I could be there for the kids. Dean was cremated, and they had a memorial service. Beth, Anna, and Autumn were there too. He and Anna were close. She considered him her brother. He was in an accident some time before his death and came into some money. He made Anna his power of attorney. He was still with Rita after all these years, and they had two kids. At the time of his death, Evan was ten and Holly was fourteen.

I told Eugene once summer was over we could move back home. For working at the condominiums during the busy summer, we always got a nice bonus. I didn't want to leave the job shorthanded in the busy season, and the bonus was a nice addition.

Lana came to move in with us for a little while. She knew we were planning to move back and could use a change of scenery for a while. I helped her get a job working the front desk at another set of condominiums the property management owned.

I took her to Goodwill, and she bought herself twelve outfits for around $65. I taught the girl how to bargain shop. Seemed like she was very responsible with her money. She was going to ride back and forth to work with me and save money to buy her a car before she moved back home.

I had put my notice in for the middle of October since we didn't get the summer bonuses until the first of October.

Trisha was admitted into the hospital, so Eugene and I drove up to see her. She was awake and talking. One thing she said to Rory was that he and Kara were going to have two more kids. We stayed the night at Rory and Kara's and drove back home the next day.

When it came time to move back home, we had packed everything up in boxes and gone to rent the U-Haul. Before we had the chance to start loading it, we received a call from Kara. Trisha had gotten worse since we left from visiting. We decided to take the U-Haul back for now and just go see her instead.

I prayed, "Dear Lord, thank you for putting Trisha in our lives. Please don't take her yet. How will we go on without her? She has such a caring heart and so many people that care about her. Please take us safely to her. I ask this be your will. In Jesus's name, amen."

We made it safely to the facility that she was in. She was resting peacefully, but she knew we were there. I could tell. I went to her bedside, kissed her forehead, and told her that I loved her so much. She was the best mother-in-law a girl could have. I was honored to be her daughter-in-law. I talked to her like I would normally. Told her Lana just came back home the other day. That she had been working at some other condominiums on the beach and bought herself a car. She really liked Lana. I'd never seen them together that she wasn't laughing at her about something. She said that she was very comical.

We went to stay at Rory and Kara's for the night. Exhausted from the trip and the mental stress, we fell asleep quickly.

Rory knocked on the bedroom door about six-thirty the next morning. He came in and told us that their mom had passed away a few minutes ago. Oh, how that hurt me. I knew Eugene and Rory had to really be hurting.

They would have so many memories of her to share. I am so blessed to have known her like I did. We talked on the phone a lot when we could. I would miss our talks. She was in heaven now with her mother and father. What a reunion that was! I prayed for God to wrap his loving arms around us and give us strength to get through this. It would not be easy. That was for sure. Denae was there too. She had been staying with Dane and Trisha for some time now, helping to take care of her. Olivia, Katie, and Aiden were living with their dad in Missouri.

We stayed in town until after Trisha's funeral. Oh, what a beautiful service. Rory gave a eulogy, and I don't see how he made it through it. It made everyone cry.

Once we got home, I went back to work. The property management company would not let me stay on with the current property as Sage's office manager. They sent me to another property on the other side of town as an assistant manager.

Rory helped us pay one more month of rent where we were living. Then we found a little place on the other side of town. It was a step down from where we were living, but we would make it work.

I worked there for about a month, and the manager quit, so they asked me to be the interim general manager, and they gave me a nice raise, which was good because it was a much bigger and older property than where I was.

I really missed working with Sage and hated working at this old property. The employees were nice, and that was about all I liked about it The property management company kept promising for me to be transferred to another property that included a two-bedroom two-bath apartment with my salary. They just kept saying they had to wait to let the current manager go.

Until then I was stuck here where I dreaded going to work every day. They finally hired a general manager but wanted me as assistant general manager until after summer.

I had to attend all the manager meetings and board meetings. I also got stuck with all the project bids and overseeing the contractors. This was all general manager duties. I barely had time for my own reports.

I prayed for God to give me patience and allow it to all to work out as it should. I had to put my faith in him and believe he had a plan for me.

In early August 2017, the general manager was hospitalized with liver failure. He was going to be out a while and we had a board meeting this month, so I had to do all reports and speech. I was extremely nervous because the board members were tough.

I survived the meeting, and the day after it wasn't looking too good here. The weather was looking bad, and we were tracking a hurricane coming our way. All our family members were calling to check on us. Lacy came down for a visit and just left the day before. I was so glad she made it home.

On the morning of August 24, a hurricane warning was issued for our town. I had to go to work and make sure we had everything secured before Eugene and I could leave. By noon, a mandatory evacuation was in place.

My phone was blowing up with texts from family members, asking me if I was leaving. I told them as soon as I finished securing the condominiums I could leave. Mama was extremely worried. I assured her that we would have plenty of time to leave before the hurricane made it.

Finally, around four-thirty that afternoon I was able to go home and help Eugene pack up some of our things. We had the truck cab filled tight, and the car was full except room for us to sit.

We took the truck inland and parked it so we could ride together in the car. The Daltons had arranged for us to spend the night in a hotel four hours away. Almost halfway home. We were going to stay with Rory and Kara until it was safe to return to the coast.

I prayed and prayed on the way to the hotel, asking the Lord to make sure we stayed safe on the road and the town was spared from the hurricane. I was so scared. I asked the Lord to take away my fear.

We made it to the hotel. I let the Daltons know we had gotten there safely and posted that we had safely evacuated on social media. I called Mama to let her know that we had safely evacuated. Traffic had been so bad with everyone evacuating. I was so tired, but my mind would not shut off. I just lay there talking to God most of the night.

The next morning, we got up bright and early hoping to get ahead of the traffic. We grabbed some fast-food breakfast. Then we were off. The hurricane had not hit land yet. It looked like our small town was in the direct path of where it was heading.

I started praying again as Eugene drove. Please protect everyone and keep them safe. The general manager of the condominiums I worked for was still in the hospital. They had transferred him to a hospital more inland. The employees were more like family even though I did not like the property. I was in contact with all of them I could to make sure they were safe.

We made it safely to Rory and Kara's. I kept checking the hurricane center to see what was going on with the weather. About ten o'clock that evening the hurricane made it to land just north of our town. Whether or not any damage was done, we would not know until morning.

I tried to get some rest. Kara gave me some natural anxiety drops. They seem to help enough that I finally got some sleep.

I woke up to devastating news. Our small town received high wind and water damage with ten-foot wave surges in some parts of town. From what we could see on TV, it did not look good. The hurricane hit as a category 4 with highest wind speeds of 135 mph, and the storm just stalled for an exceedingly long time.

Thank God no deaths occurred in the town. Homes were destroyed, but they could be replaced, not lives.

A storm chaser was filming our town as he drove around on social media. There were boats everywhere, mostly stuck into homes or buildings. He asked for any requested drive bys. I gave them my address. As he turned down my street, I gasped all along that road. Homes were destroyed. When he made it to my house, it was partially still standing but had two boats in the side of it.

He said, "A ten-foot wave went through this neighborhood. It was the highest in the area."

I cried hysterically and thanked God that we had gotten out of there. We had tried to get all the sentimental nonreplaceable items from our home when we evacuated. I saw an aerial shot of the condominiums I managed. It was flooded badly with most sliding glass doors blown out. The property I worked for with Sage looked like one side had been hit badly. The assistant maintenance manager had to stay there during the storm. I hoped and prayed he was safe.

They gave the okay for town citizens to return to their homes to collect belongings and assess damages. Eugene and I got on the road. We stopped inland to pick up the truck first. It was fine. Thank you, Lord! No broken windows or leaks. We had to be out by seven o'clock that evening according to curfew.

The boats had been pulled away from the house when we arrived. The roof was full of holes, and even though the house was off the ground, there was still mud and a high waterline inside. Oh, and the stench was awful. I busted into tears immediately upon entering. I thought about my biological mother's wedding dress that I had left in the second bedroom closet. It was still there thankfully. However, there was at least a foot of mud on it. Probably ruined.

I was unable to be in what was left of the house long enough to hold it together. Eugene went through everything by himself pretty much. Then when we got ready to leave, the truck would not start. The neighbor called someone for us, and he got it started after several minutes but would not accept money for his help. That was one of God's angels. He just said, "We all must come together in times like this to help one another."

I needed to stop by the condominiums and pick up a few things. I called to see if anyone was there, and the board president and an employee from the property management company were. I told them that I needed to talk to them. Also, I had the petty cash bag and my keys to turn in. I let them know that my home was scheduled for demolition the next day. I handed them the bag and my keys and said, "Thank you for the opportunity I had here in South Texas and the experience I had gained from the position. Unfortunately, I no longer have a home, so my husband and I are going to move in with some family back in Central Texas." All he said was, "Okay, well, stay in touch with us."

We were loaded up and heading back to Rory and Kara's house. Eugene was in the truck, and I was following in the car. I was nervous since I had never driven that far alone. I prayed, thanking God that we had made it out safely and for saving most of our sentimental items that were in the house during the hurricane. None of the furniture was salvageable, but that's all replaceable. The main thing was we were alive and safe.

It was sad driving through the destroyed town. It didn't even look like the same place we had lived for a little over four years. It was probably going to take some time to rebuild the town.

I called Mama to let her know that we were safe and on our way back north. I also let Kara know we were heading back to their house.

I was so relieved when we made it to Rory and Kara's. It was good to see their kids. They were a nice distraction to reality. They were so full of joy and innocence.

While they were so nice to let us stay with them, I tried helping as much as possible. We would watch the kids when needed, cook dinner, wash dishes, help with homework, and anything other ways we could help.

We took my mom's wedding dress to the cleaners. I told the lady that the dress was my mother's, fifty years old, and was badly stained from the hurricane. She said to leave it with her and she would do her best to get it out. After we left, she called to tell us that the man in line behind us wanted to pay for the cleaning. He was another angel here on earth.

She called us a few days later to let us know it was ready. We went to pick it up. I cried tears of joy once I saw it. It was cleaner and more beautiful to me than it had been all the years that I had it.

Chapter Sixty-One

We were able to get some help with FEMA for things we lost. I was ready to go back to our hometown to be closer to Lacy and Lana. David was now stationed in Iowa.

Eugene's dad, Dane, said we could stay in his house. That's where Eugene grew up and only four miles from Mama's house. I took some time and visited friends and family I hadn't seen in a while. I found out Uncle Jean was preaching at a small church about fifteen miles from the house, so I started going there on Sundays.

Aunt Elsa was living with her son, Joe, about forty-five minutes away. I went to visit them as much as possible. David came into town, and we all went out there. Anna and her kids met us there too. Aunt Elsa was so happy to see everyone.

I found out Beth was sick with cancer. She only lived about five minutes from us. I went to visit her at least once or twice a week. Autumn and her two boys were living with her. I would take Beth to the doctor if she needed a ride and cooked dinner for them. Autumn and Leena both worked, so I helped when they weren't off.

It was nice being so close to the girls again too. I saw them at least once a week. Lacy was at Beth's on her days off, helping her out and watching their favorite TV shows. I was still helping as much as possible too. Autumn was working full-time, plus taking care of Beth, cooking and cleaning. I would call Beth during the week or go by and see if she needed anything.

Leena was able to rent a house so close to Beth's that their backyards were only separated by a fence. I was relieved that she was nearby if Beth needed her.

Something was going on with me. Even being so close to all my family and friends, I was so depressed and always angry at Eugene. I would have emotional outbursts for no reason. I'd pray to God to help me work through whatever it was that was happening to me. I began to have nightmares and wake myself up screaming, or Eugene would wake me up because I was crying in my sleep.

I got to the point I was scared to go to sleep at night because most nights I had nightmares about J.R. there and trying to hurt me. This went on for about a month, and I decided it was time to get some help.

I called around looking for a therapist. They were all so expensive. There was no way that I could afford therapy. I had left a message with a Christian counseling center. I prayed so hard for God to help me. I was so depressed and shaking all the time. I hadn't felt suicidal in years, but I had that feeling again. I just wanted to die but really didn't know why.

A couple of days later, a psychologist returned my call from there. Her name was Jennifer, and she asked me to come in the next day for a free evaluation.

I got up and got ready to go meet with Jennifer. I felt very comfortable with her right away. She and her office were both so warm and welcoming. I felt that I could tell her anything. At the end of our hour, she told me that she believed I had PTSD and major depressive disorder. For some unknown reason, she felt like the hurricane brought back longtime repressed feelings and memories. She agreed to see me free for six visits, and after that, we could work out something.

On the way home, I thanked God so much for sending her to me. He knew I needed help to work through all this. I had just pushed it down for all these years, and things just kept piling up. I was going to therapy as a teenager, but my dad had pulled me out once I was pregnant with Lacy, so feelings never were resolved.

Six visits later I was feeling a little better. At the end of the visit, I asked Jennifer, "This is my sixth visit, how much will the visits be because I want to keep seeing you?" Her answer to me was, "Nothing. God wants me to keep seeing you too. You are special to him, and he has sent you to me. We will just keep doing what we are doing."

I had felt that God had sent me to her too, but I never imagined this. She was indeed an earth angel. I honestly believe that when you are being pulled under in the quicksand, that God sends someone to pull you out. This time it was Jennifer.

Late November, I began to have horrible back pain. I could feel my back spasming. I also noticed I was a little unbalanced, almost tripping over my own feet at times.

I continued to go to counseling with Jennifer, and the nightmares were coming further and further apart. That told me that talking with her was a big help. She always had good ideas. Some I really liked was shooting pictures of J.R. with a BB gun and writing him a letter and then burning it. I learned from speaking to her that I was also angry at my dad. I wrote him a three-page letter and went to his grave to read it to him. After that, I yelled at him.

I went to visit Aunt Elsa at Joe's. She and I were talking while sitting on the porch with Joe. She asked, "J.R. did bad things to you when you were growing up, didn't he?" I looked at Joe, and he was looking at me.

I answered her, "Yes, he did."

Joe asked, "What kind of bad things?"

I just started to cry and told him. He couldn't believe my daddy knew about it and didn't believe me. Aunt Elsa said it was true because she caught him.

I continued to see Jennifer. Seemed like I always went to see her right after a bad day. That's how I knew God put her in my life. I had Eugene go with me once so he could get a better idea of what I was going through. He was going to try to help me as much as he possibly could.

January 2018, I finally had health insurance. Jennifer was going to recommend that I take an antidepressant and sent a note to the doctor with my diagnosis.

When I got in to see the doctor, she also gave me an antianxiety prescription and a muscle relaxer for my back spasms. They seemed to help with the pain and sleep for a little while. Then she had to up the dosage on the muscle relaxers, some Tylenol with codeine, and took me off the anxiety meds.

Eugene got a job working as a maintenance man for a pharmaceutical company. He was off every weekend but on call every few. He seemed to like his job, and his boss liked him as well as the employees. He did have a lot of responsibilities, which would overwhelm him at times.

I prayed to God for every day he gave me. I asked his forgiveness for my sins and to lead me to a job allowing me to work from home, as I believed this was the job he sent to me.

I started working a remote position as a reservationist for resorts in

Myrtle Beach. There were twenty-one resorts that I had to learn about and make reservations for. I really enjoyed being able to work from home, although it didn't allow much time to help Beth out.

We basically got to make our own schedules but with restrictions. They would give you a total of minimum hours that you had to work, a minimum number of evening shifts, and so many weekend hours to work. We would get two fifteen-minute breaks if you worked an eight-hour shift with a fifteen-minute lunch break. Anything less than eight hours, you only got one fifteen-minute break and lunch. I liked working split shifts so I could do yoga on my two-hour break and check on Beth.

CHAPTER SIXTY-TWO

In October Kara had another baby girl. They named her Ariel. She had cotton-white hair and blue eyes. Just like Rory when he was young. If Trisha was right, they still had one more child to have.

A year later, I had continued to see Jennifer on my weekdays off. We both agreed that it didn't seem the antidepressant was working as well anymore. I told the doctor this at my next appointment. She changed me to another prescription.

About a month later, I woke up for work, and Eugene was getting ready for work. I told him I didn't feel right and was going to lie back down for a minute. I had a seizure, and he took me to the hospital.

They ran several tests but couldn't find anything. I took a couple of days off because I was very weak. I made an appointment with my doctor, and she referred me to a neurologist.

Before I could get into see the neurologist, I had another seizure. I gave a medication list to him, and there was one he didn't think I needed and switched it. He prescribed an anti-seizure medication and put me on a different antidepressant. He had me walk up and down the hall and noticed I wasn't swinging my arms normally, and my gait was a little off, and he just asked Eugene, "Why is she walking like that?"

I prayed for God to make me better and take care of my family, including Aunt Elsa, which wasn't doing too well. I asked him to send me to a more knowledgeable specialist.

When I followed up with my doctor, she referred me to a psychiatrist. The next visit I had with Jennifer, I told her about the referral. She had heard of Dr. Bristol and thought he was a great psychiatrist. She said some of her other patients see him for meds and her for the therapy.

I went to see Dr. Bristol. He was very confused why I was recently on an antipsychotic medication, and I never should have been on it. He changed my antidepressant again and added an antianxiety prescription for me. He could tell I was very anxious.

Thanking God was an everyday occurrence. He had helped me to get better. Since I was no longer on the antipsychotic drug, there were no more seizures. Dr. Bristol was put in my path to take care of that, and it seemed the medications he had me on were making a difference. I only had to see him every four months now if I kept seeing Jennifer. That would not be a problem. After all she was my earth angel.

I had received a promotion from work since I made New Hire of the Year. I was now a team leader. I went back to working eight-hour shifts with a thirty-minute break. However, it wasn't long until I realized how they were taking advantage of me. I was being left to manage the whole remote staff for four hours at a time alone. That was like fifty to sixty employees at once by chat on the computer. It was stressing me out.

I asked God to send me a sign if I should look for another job from home. I told him that I could not the stress that this job inflicted on me. I could tell that it had me snapping at Eugene, and he didn't deserve it. I also wanted to know if I should see a different primary doctor.

I had recently gone to part-time working. I just couldn't sit in that chair for so many hours at a time. I liked my part-time schedule better and got a longer break in between shifts. I was able to work on my yoga as best I could.

July 3, 2019, Autumn called me early that morning to let me know her mom, Beth, had passed away peacefully during the night. She was no longer suffering.

God is so amazing to answer my prayers again. I had faith that he sent me another job from home for pest control. Starting on my birthday was a sure sign. Also, Eugene's uncle Ray recommended I go see his primary doctor. I made an appointment with him.

The doctor was worried about me, and my balance was worsening as well as my gait. He scheduled me for an MRI and referred me to a neurologist two hours away.

Before I got in to see him—it was 2020—I had a couple of bad falls, one that I ended up having to go by ambulance to the hospital and needed a few staples in my head. He had received copies of all my CTs and MRIs. I had to walk up and down the hall, and then we went back to his exam room. It was then he diagnosed me with Parkinson's. Eugene and I were in total shock. He prescribed me Sinemet. All it did was make me so sick to my stomach constantly.

My calls for work were being timed, and I couldn't put in the necessary information into the system in time. I couldn't get in and out of the chair without Eugene's help. He brought a bedside toilet in and put next to my desk. My hand was double-clicking the mouse or keys. I had to stop working. I just wasn't physically able to do it any longer.

He saw me again and ordered physical therapy and changed the medication dosage. He also filled out some paperwork for my disability application. A month later he put me on a different medication, and all I wanted to do was sleep. He scheduled me for a PET scan, and when he got those results, he did a virtual appointment with me. It was then he told me he really didn't know what was going on with me. He referred me to a couple of movement disorder specialists.

Lana got me a little puppy since I was so depressed. He was a toy rat terrier, and I named him Snoopy. Smartest puppy I had ever seen. He was puppy pad trained in under two weeks.

March 23, Lacy called me to let me know that Autumn had taken her own life. Oh, how this saddened me. She was there for me when I wanted to take my life and stopped me. Why had she not come to talk to me or Anna? I had to call Anna. Autumn was her best friend for over thirty-five years. Anna said she was just over at her house the night before and told her that she would not take her own life. I had to pray for her sons right away. How abandoned they must feel. I could not imagine.

Now with Covid-19 everywhere, I was scared to go to a doctor's office out of town, or physical therapy, so I turned down the appointments. That was until I just couldn't. I got worse very quickly.

May 2021 I started going to aquatic therapy before I could get an appointment with a specialist. I had to call them to come get me from the car in a wheelchair. The physical therapist, named Tye, timed me in an evaluation with a walker. It took me over a minute using a walker to get thirty-nine feet. He had to use the lift chair to get me in and out of the pool. Cooper, the sweet receptionist, would push me out to the car if Tye had another patient.

A month later, thanks to Tye's motivation and my determination, I was walking into the building with Eugene's assistance and up the steps to get in and out of the pool. Cooper became my personal cheerleader. The whole crew really did a great job of making you feel welcome.

CHAPTER SIXTY-THREE

I went to a spinal clinic and had an epidural done on my back. Then my neck started giving me a lot of problems. I would cry from being in so much pain.

I prayed for the Lord to please take this awful pain away every night so I could get some sleep. The spinal clinic did an epidural on my neck. I remained pain-free for one week.

I started praying, "God, just please take me home. I am so tired of hurting like this. I just want to sleep and wake up in heaven with you. Please, take me." I begged him. I wanted to die so I wouldn't be in any pain anymore.

I got a letter from the Social Security Administration telling me I was eligible for disability. I would receive back pay all the way from February.

After two months of physical therapy, I had an appointment scheduled with a movement disorder specialist. It was almost three hours away and at eight o'clock in the morning, so I reserved a pet-friendly cabin close by the office at a reasonable rate. Mama was going to go with us so she could go to the appointment with me. She was a nurse, and I wanted her to make sure we understood everything, and Eugene would stay at the cabin with Snoopy.

Two weeks before my appointment, I had severe neck pain. It felt like a Charlie Horse in my neck. I had Eugene rub Biofreeze on it constantly, and I would take muscle relaxers. I could not relax and was always very tense and had lost so much weight.

I could not take it anymore, so I had Eugene take me to Urgent Care. The doctor there gave me some pain medicine, something for nausea, and muscle relaxer by IV. Eugene said it was the most relaxed he had seen me in months. The doctor ordered a CT. When the report came in, the doctor said I had torticollis also known as wryneck. The radiologist could see the spasms in the CT.

It was the best that I had felt in months. I went home and slept for hours, thanking God for taking my pain away and allowing me to finally be able to sleep all night.

I remained pain-free for one more week. Then it was back worse than ever. I screamed out in pain. Mama came over and gave me a different cream to try out and massaged my neck. It helped for about thirty minutes, but then the pain came back.

I prayed again for God to take me home. I could not stand it. All I wanted to do was die. It hurt so bad. I was still talking to Jennifer. That helped me emotionally, but I needed physical help too.

I was still going to physical therapy, and Tye gave me some neck stretches to do hoping they would help. Unfortunately, they did not.

Eugene had to take me back to Urgent Care. The doctor gave me some morphine by IV along with more muscle relaxers. She kept me for a couple of hours to observe me. I went to sleep; I was so exhausted.

Dr. Williams, the movement disorder specialist, came highly recommended. The day of the appointment, we got to the clinic, found a parking spot in the parking garage. Mama pushed me in my wheelchair to Dr. Williams's office and completed the paperwork. Right as Mama turned it in, the nurse called me back to the exam room. She took my vitals and said the doctor would be right in.

As soon as the nurse left the room, Dr. Williams came in and introduced herself. She reviewed my chart and referral paperwork. Then she did her own physical examination. She had me get out of my wheelchair and do some walking around and turning around, checked my reflexes and a couple of other things. When we asked her if she believed it was Parkinson's, she replied, "No, I am leaning more to MSA, or what is known as multi system atrophy."

I asked her if I would get better, and she told me no, that there was no cure. She ordered a couple of tests and lab work. She also wanted me to start on a prescription. Parkinsonism was associated with the MSA.

She stayed with us for two and a half hours total through the examination. We left the exam room and went to the lab. Mama was going to the pharmacy to pick up the sample prescription that Dr. Williams called in while I was getting the test and lab work done.

I called Eugene to let him know what was taking so long and that Dr. Williams said I did not have Parkinson's.

He asked, "What is it then?"

I replied, "She believes it is MSA. I need to call the office to let them know we will be a little later checking out. I will see you soon."

I called the owner of the cabin to tell her that the appointment took longer than we thought it would. She told me that was fine, and she would let the housekeeper know.

Dr. Williams had called in some pain medicine for me and scheduled me to come back in a month for Botox injections in my neck. I had the lab work and test done, and Mama picked up the prescription.

When we arrived at the cabin to pick up Eugene and Snoopy, he came running out to Mama's truck. He was quite pale and frantic.

Mama said, "It took longer than we ever imagined. She was a great doctor though."

Eugene did not say anything. He just kept looking at me.

I asked, "What's wrong?" He still said nothing, just stared at me. "What's wrong?" I asked again.

Finally, he said, "What do you mean what's wrong? You only have five to seven years to live."

I had not had a chance to research MSA. Mama told Eugene, "She is not sure that it is MSA. It is only what she believes it to be. We have to remain positive and see what the medicine does."

Eugene was quiet the whole ride home. He just lay down on the seat and stared blanky into space. We stopped at a fast-food drive-thru on the way home, but Eugene did not want anything.

We had to go to another pharmacy to pick up my pain medication since it was a narcotic. Mama was going to work after this long day. She worked all the time. Every time they called her in on her day off, she was a devoted employee and would go in.

Her husband, Richard, had been in a nursing home for a couple of years with Parkinson's. Mama knew what I had was not Parkinson's because I had progressed so quickly.

The next month we went back to see Dr. Williams for my Botox injections. It was a later appointment, so we just drove the three-hour trip that morning. I teased that I was getting Botox for my forty-eighth birthday since it was only five days away.

Eugene and Snoopy waited at the truck while Mama pushed me in my wheelchair to the doctor's office. We checked in and sat in the lobby to be called back. Dr. Williams came and sat down with us and said she had an intern with her today, introduced us, then said she was going to review how much Botox that my insurance had approved and be right with us.

Not even five minutes had passed before we were called back to the exam room. Dr. Williams asked me several questions and examined me again. When I asked her what she thought the diagnosis was, she said that she was pretty certain it was MSA.

She got everything set up for the injections. Then she turned my wheelchair around. She touched me in every spot that she was going to inject. She injected a total of six places. One on each side of the jaw to stop drooling. One on each side of the base of the skull and one on each side of the neck.

Once again, she visited with me for a total of two and a half hours. She was very personable. I really liked this doctor, and so did Mama. I was glad Mama was with me because I really broke down in the office after Dr. Williams told us she was certain that I had MSA.

When we got back to the parking garage, I could not even look at Eugene. I knew that he was going to be upset. When we saw him, he asked what was wrong. I could not hold back, so I began to cry, telling him that she said it was MSA.

We drove back home mostly in silence. This time I was in shock. When we got home, Eugene lay on the floor next to the couch where I was lying. He rarely left my side. I asked him if we could go to Florida. It was somewhere I always wanted to go to see white sandy beaches and turquoise waters. He said we could go wherever I wanted.

I had a phone appointment with Jennifer the next day. I told her about my diagnosis. She helped me deal with it a little better by saying, "I know it is not good or what you wanted to hear, but you finally have an answer." It was true, and I knew that God would be there for me every step of the way.

I had a dream that this bright ball of light was shining, and this brighter ring of light was around that another brighter ring, and it just kept going on and on and got brighter and brighter. Then a set of praying hands came out and stretched out wide. A voice I know was God's said to me, "My child, your time is near, but first you must tell your story from the beginning."

After that message, I felt my body being lifted high. I woke up, or at least I thought I did. I was lying on my back in the air. Then I jerked awake.

We were also planning to take a trip back to South Texas in September to visit the Daltons, Nancy and Sage. Lori was going to let us stay in her condominium. I only wish that I could see her too while we were there. I visited Rhonda some before we left.

I wanted to go to Vermont in mid-October to visit Rachelle and Brad so Eugene could meet them and to see the beautiful fall colors up north.

Snoopy had begun to go get Eugene for me when I needed help. We had not even trained him to do this. I would shout out "Honey," and Snoopy would go wherever Eugene was barking and run back toward me so Eugene knew that I needed him. He was like my little service dog that trained himself.

I talked to Kara and told her our plans. We had never been on a trip together. She asked me if I would like to make it a family trip. That sounded like a great idea to me, making more memories to share. She told me to ask Mama if she would like to go since she was always such a help to me.

Rory, Kara, Boyce, Ariel, Mama, Eugene, and I went to Florida for four nights. Bryan and Avery were going to stay with Kara's parents, so they did not miss school. Rory and Kara rented a waterside house with four bedrooms and a boat. It was beautiful in Florida. I could not believe I was there. This was something I could now cross off my bucket list. I hoped going to Hawaii could be one of those things too.

We went out in the boat every day sightseeing, swimming, watching for dolphins, manatees, and eating at some really great restaurants. I was so glad that Mama got to come with us. She really deserved a vacation as much as she worked. I felt that she and I had become closer than we had ever been. I really liked that.

I got a chance to get Ariel to know me. I gained her trust, and she would get in the hot tub and pool with me. She was such a sweet girl. This trip was something that we all really needed, a break from reality.

CHAPTER SIXTY-FOUR

In October I had an appointment with Dr. Williams's assistant. Eugene stayed home, and Mama and I drove the long drive alone since it was a later appointment. Sarah, the assistant, came in and examined me. She agreed with Dr. Williams on the MSA diagnosis. She wanted a speech therapist to come up and see me.

The speech therapist had me eat a couple of things, and she felt my neck as I swallowed. She believed that I needed further testing. Since we lived so far away, she wanted to schedule a test on the same day I had my next appointment with Dr. Williams. I was scheduled another Botox appointment in November, so the speech therapist scheduled me for that date.

I prayed to God for forgiveness where I might have sinned, asking to show me the path, to take me in the right direction and to light the way for me. I wanted to do right by him.

Rachelle had gotten sick, so it looked like we were going to have to cancel our Vermont trip. I was so disappointed because I wanted Eugene and Brad to meet. I also wanted Eugene to see the pretty fall-colored mountains.

One day after physical therapy we drove by the big town church on our way home. On the marquee there was an announcement that Kirk Cameron was coming in two weeks. I said, "Kirk Cameron is coming to town. I have always wanted to meet him."

A week later, Eugene asked me, "Since we aren't going to Vermont, would you like to go see Kirk Cameron?"

I asked, "Are you serious?"

He answered, "Sure, if you want to, why not?"

I got on the computer and bought two VIP tickets to Kirk Cameron's Campfire Revival. Then Eugene asked if I wanted to see if my mama wanted to go with me. I called her and asked her. She happily accepted. I was so excited!

I had Eugene help me pick something out to wear. I could not wait for the day. I changed my mind about what to wear several times after going on video with Kaye for help.

Finally, the day arrived. Mama pushed me in my wheelchair to the security guards checking VIP tickets. We showed our tickets, and they gave us our lanyards. Then we went into the auditorium where the stage was. She pushed me to the front row and set my brakes. After a few moments, Kirk came out onto the stage. There was a question-and-answer session, and then everyone lined up for pictures with him. I just sat there in my wheelchair. I waited off stage for him to take a picture with me.

It was better than that though. For a moment I felt like I was on "Make a Wish." Two men from the audience offered to put my wheelchair on stage. I told Kirk I wanted to take my picture standing next to him. He held my hands to help me out of the chair and helped me walk to the photo background. He allowed me to hold on to his arm while I stood next to him for a picture, and I gave him a bracelet with Defeat MSA website on it.

I waited on stage in my chair until the men that put me on stage had their turn for a picture so they could bring me back down off stage. Next there was a thirty-minute break before Kirk came out to speak to everyone including non-VIP guests. I loved hearing him speak and hearing him talk about the national monument to the forefathers. It starts with Faith. She stands upon a main pedestal, one foot resting upon a replica of Plymouth Rock, and holds an open Bible in her left hand. Her right hand points to heaven. The symbolism is trust in God and his words written down for us in the Bible. Four smaller, seated figures represent the Christian values and principles made known by the Pilgrims themselves. They are Morality, Law, Education, and Liberty.

Morality holds the Ten Commandments in her left hand and the scroll of Revelation (the last book of the Bible) in the right. She is surrounded by an Old Testament prophet on one side and the evangelists on the other. Law is with Justice on the one hand and Mercy on the other. Education is with the Wisdom of maturity on one side with Youth and Experience on the other. Liberty is companied by Peace on the one side and the Overthrow of Tyranny on the opposite side.

After Kirk spoke on stage, we went outside by campfires. There we heard some great Christian music, and he spoke a little more.

Before Mama and I left, I asked a security guard if I could speak to Kirk. He walked over to me in my wheelchair. I asked him if he would sign my ticket. He signed it as we talked about my diagnosis.

He asked, "Can I pray for you?"

I replied, "Of course."

He knelt beside me and held my hands as he prayed. Afterward, I said, "God had spoken to me."

He asked, "What did he say?"

I answered, "That my time was near, but I have to tell my story first."

He asked, "How do you plan to do that?"

I answered, "I think that maybe I should write a book."

He thought that was a great idea and told me to keep him updated and gave me an email address so I could.

Thanks to Kirk Cameron, I began to write this book the very next day. It had been something that I had thought about doing for some time, but now I had the motivation and willpower to do so.

Special Thanks to Kirk Cameron!

God put you in my path for a reason. We were planning to go on a trip to Vermont and visit a friend the week that I met you. Then my friend became ill, and our plans were cancelled. As my husband and I drove by the big church in our town one day, I saw on the marquee that you were coming to our town on your American Campfire tour.

My husband asked me later if I would like to go see you since our plans were cancelled. I exclaimed, "Of course, I have always wanted to meet him!" Immediately I purchased two tickets. One for me and one for my stepmother, that attended with me and pushed me in my wheelchair.

Thank you for taking the time to speak with me and pray for me. That truly meant so much. During our talk I told you that God had spoke to me and said that my time was near, but I had to share my story from the beginning first. You asked me how I planned to do that.

I had thought about it in the past, but never moved forward. By the Grace of God, you gave me the inspiration and motivation I needed to write this book. You are another one of the Earth Angels put here by God. Now my story can be read by others who struggle with the same kind of situations, and hopefully be of help to them. I can't thank you enough.

God Bless You!
Daisy Paige

What is Multiple System Atrophy? (MSA) is a rare, degenerative neurological disorder affecting your body's involuntary (autonomic) functions, including blood pressure, breathing, bladder function and motor control. MSA shares many Parkinson's disease-like symptoms, such as slow movement, rigid muscles and poor balance. Treatment includes medications and lifestyle changes to help manage symptoms, but there is no cure. The condition progresses gradually and eventually leads to death.

Multiple system atrophy (MSA) affects many parts of your body. Symptoms typically develop in adulthood, usually in the 50s or 60s. It is classified by two types: parkinsonian and cerebellar. The type depends on the symptoms you have at diagnosis.

Parkinsonian type
This is the most common type of MSA. The signs and symptoms are similar to those of Parkinson's disease, such as:
- Rigid muscles
- Difficulty bending your arms and legs
- Slow movement (bradykinesia)
- Tremors (rare in MSA compared with classic Parkinson's disease)
- Problems with posture and balance

Cerebellar type
The main signs and symptoms are problems with muscle coordination (ataxia), but others may include
- Impaired movement and coordination, such as unsteady gait and loss of balance
- Slurred, slow or low-volume speech (dysarthria)
- Visual disturbances, such as blurred or double vision and difficulty focusing your eyes
- Difficulty swallowing (dysphagia) or chewing

You can also develop dangerously high blood pressure levels while lying down (supine hypertension).
MSA might cause other difficulties with involuntary (autonomic) body functions, including:
Urinary and bowel dysfunction, Sweating abnormalities, Sleep

disorders, Sexual dysfunction, Cardiovascular problems and Psychiatric problems.

10% of all book proceeds will go to www.defeatmsa.org/donate-to-us/, it is a US based 501(c)(3) national charity that aspires to balance support for patients, education of medical professionals, raising public awareness, nurturing promising research and advocacy for the MSA community. You can also help by donating directly from the information located on the website. All donations go to researching for a cure or treatments to help those diagnosed with MSA.

"We remain committed to the care of all those challenged by this devastating disease wherever they are in the world and in whatever way MSA appears. As that old civil rights commandment says, "If not us, then who? If not now, then when?" We must do what we can to alleviate the suffering of others and to combat this disease in whatever way we can."

Phillip M. Fortier
Founding Director, Defeat MSA Alliance

The Lord's Prayer

Our Father, who art in heaven,
hallowed be thy name,
thy kingdom come,
thy will be done,
on Earth as it is in heaven.

Give us this day our daily bread.
And forgive us our trespasses,
as we forgive those
who trespass against us.

And lead us not into temptation,
but deliver us from evil.

For thine is the kingdom,
and the power, and the glory,
for ever and ever.
Amen.

CPSIA information can be obtained
at www.ICGtesting.com
Printed in the USA
LVHW101001220722
724154LV00011B/44